CW00494288

RUPERT BRISTOW

999 PRAYERS

for most occasions and situations

kevin mayhew

www.kevinmayhew.com

kevin
mayhew

First published in Great Britain in 2015 by Kevin Mayhew Ltd
Buxhall, Stowmarket, Suffolk IP14 3BW
Tel: +44 (0) 1449 737978 Fax: +44 (0) 1449 737834
E-mail: info@kevinmayhew.com

www.kevinmayhew.com

9 8 7 6 5 4 3 2 1 0

ISBN 978 1 84867 782 1
Catalogue No. 1501478

Cover design by Justin Minns
© Image used under licence from Shutterstock Inc.
Typesetting by Angela Selfe

Printed and bound in Great Britain

For Sarah, as always, and our sons, Michael and Richard

For Canon John Tapper,
my former vicar, who has always encouraged my writing

Contents

About the author

Rupert Bristow, a Reader in Trinity Benefice, Folkestone, is the author of seven books of prayers for Kevin Mayhew and was Director of Education for Canterbury Diocese from 1995 until his retirement in 2008. He has taught on VSO in Rwanda, was the second Director of the UK Council for Overseas Student Affairs, and then Dean of Student Services at London South Bank University. He has also been a specialist adviser to a House of Commons select committee, edited and written for various educational publications and chaired Kent SACRE (Standing Advisory Council for Religious Education). He is an Honorary Fellow of Canterbury Christ Church University and is currently a governor of East Kent College and a member of the Discipleship and Spirituality Resource Group in Canterbury Diocese.

Introduction

This book of prayers is both a collection and a resource. A collection because most of the prayers here are drawn from my previous books (listed at the end), though it also includes pages written especially for this volume, some at the suggestion of people who have felt the need for particular subjects to be covered, for example vestry prayers. Yet I hope people will see it as a resource when prayers are needed for special occasions and in particular situations, for example in schools, as well as for worship in church, at various kinds of meetings and for personal use.

So, whether you are preparing next Sunday's intercessions, want a suitable grace to say at a special celebration, or just need some refreshment for your daily prayers, you should find something here to suit you – or prompt you to write something better!

I am grateful to the many people who have given me helpful feedback on the kind of prayers people are searching for. Above all, though, I pray that the words I am given and the prayers that I write will enable me and all who dip into this book to have a closer connection to the God whose gifts we share day by day.

Rupert Bristow

'ARROW' PRAYERS

(Short prayers for personal use in emergencies and in challenging or difficult situations.)

1 Lord, hear our intercessions as we listen to your word.

2 Let us know the mind of Christ,
as well as feel his love.

3 Make us whole,
in body and soul.

4 Give me hope in the darkness, Lord,
and consolation in my sorrow.

5 May our joy never be at another's expense.

6 May our sorrows be shared
by friends who care, including your Son.

7 Immanent God, always on hand,
guide me all the days of my life.

8 Lord, help me to hope, teach me to trust.
Above all, Lord, may I see you more clearly, day by day.

9 Bring me sleep to refresh my body.
Bring me peace to refresh my soul.

10 Let it be you, Lord, to grant me your peace.
Let it be me, Lord, to give you my heart.

11 Send me out to preach your word and save a soul.

12 May I survive the test and give you my best.

13 Lord, with you there is no mission impossible.

14 Let me go along your way, not mine.

15 Keep me from harm, keep others safe.

16 Lord, may our journey bring great expectation
and our arrival great joy.

17 Watch over me as I grow spiritually.
Top up my energy and refresh my search for truth.

18 Bring me sun to cheer me.
Send me rain to cool me.

19 Guide my footsteps, please Lord,
both uphill and downhill.

20 Let healing do its work
and wholeness be the outcome,
by your grace, not my faith.

21 As nature provides, your love guides.

22 May this church flourish, if it is your wish.

23 God of purpose, show us your will.
God of mission, send us out to serve.

24 Give me the will to keep going
and the energy to complete the task.

25 Create in me, Lord,
the desire to do your will.

26 Lord of surprise and grace,
thank you for helping me to take this risk.

27 As I travel,
let me be more like a pilgrim,
less like a tourist.

28 Keep me safe as I travel
and grateful when I return.

29 I feel broken.
Remake me, Lord.

30 Let me serve you for saving me.

31 May Christian hope be a constant in my life;
and give me a glimpse of eternity along the way.

32 Grant me the gift of remembering
and the time and the will to record those memories.

33 Let me know your ways, Lord,
and grant me a closer walk with you
till you bring me home.

34 Hold me close, keep me safe.

35 Loving God, make me your own.

36 Guard and guide……….
Watch over *her/him/them* night and day.

37 Lord, bring me hope at the start
and even more hope at the end.

38 God help me,
God lead me,
God show me.

39 Today's a big day for me.
Make it a big day for you too, Lord.

40 Let nothing be in moderation
when we worship you.

41 Even the ordinary is extraordinary,
so let me do the small things well.

42 Empower me to do your will.
Equip me to do it well.

43 Help me to get the balance right
between family, work and you, Lord.

44 I am yours, Lord,
show me you are mine.

45 Be close, be near, take away my fear.

46 Give me the energy to prepare
and the preparedness to surprise.

47 O God, help me face my class.
Bring out the best in me and in my students.

48 Raise my sights to your horizons, Lord.

49 Jesus, be my teacher.
Jesus, be my friend.

50 Give me the power to be creative in these moments of peace.

51 Be with me as I am put to the test.
Help me to remember how your Son was tested for me.

52 Help me to be more patient with others and less impatient
with myself.

53 Lord, help me and hold me;
love me and never leave me.

54 Lord, help me to take responsibility when I need to
and to let go when you say so.

55 Bring me patience and peace when I really want to let fly.

56 It's awfully difficult just now, Lord.
Calm me with your presence, fill me with your wisdom.

57 Help me to hear in the noise and listen in the silence.

58 Help me today, Lord, to listen and to learn, and to do all you would want of me.

59 Grant me peace and integrity when the pressure is on and the going gets tough.

60 Give me the perseverance to see this task through to the end.
Thank you, Lord.

61 Watch over all involved in this operation, Lord.
Thank you for the gifts you have given them
and the skills they have learnt.

62 Help me to face this task,
knowing you are by my side.

63 May this birth be full of wonder
and the baby bring joy to the world.

64 Courage, be my friend.
Hope, be at my end.

SEASONS OF THE CHRISTIAN YEAR

Advent

65 Lord of light,
alert us to the hope of banishing darkness
so that we may be open to the coming of your Son.
May we also have our eyes opened to the end time,
ready and expectant, always prepared.
Let the energy of your mighty power
dazzle and refresh us,
as you bring us your love and peace,
mercy and grace, expectation and anticipation.
Amen

66 We pray for your Church
in its long journey in the light of Christ.
Shine your love into any dark corners,
prepare us for the glories to come,
and help us to sustain our worship and wonder.
As we look forward to the birth of your Son,
let us look back in penitence and humility,
committing ourselves anew to do your will
and to deepen our faith through worship and prayer.
Amen

67 God of light and might,
bring to our world a new beginning,
a fresh start for your people.
We give thanks for the anticipation
of promises fulfilled that John heralded.
May we rejoice in all that lies ahead,
as we move from darkness to light,
from repentance to forgiveness,
from despair to hope.
Help us to be prepared for change,
in ourselves and in your Church,
for now and for ever.
Amen

68 God of hope,
at this time we look forward in anticipation
and look back in thankfulness.
Bless all those who pave the way for others,
remembering especially the ministry of John the Baptist.
As we await the coming of the light of the world,
may we reach out to others
and bring them into the light,
out of the shadow of darkness.
Renew and restore us,
so that we can play our part
in your great mission to the world,
through your Son, Jesus Christ.
Amen

69 Loving Lord,
as we embark on the season of Advent,
help us to take stock of our faith
and to prepare the way on our own journey.
We give thanks for the promise of forgiveness,
through John's ministry of repentance through baptism,
and eagerly await the restoration of our relationship with you,
through the coming of your Son at Bethlehem.
As Mary and Joseph patiently waited,
so may we be faithful and watchful,
in our prayers and penitence.
Amen

70 Almighty God,
create in us this Advent
a sense of your presence;
a knowledge of your love;
a certainty of your hope;
and an understanding of your promise.
Shine a light in our lives
to expose our failings;
to highlight our penitence;
to renew our faith;
and to prepare us for the coming of your Son,
as John the Baptist did.
Amen

71 Almighty God,
as we begin to prepare for the wonder and mystery of Christmas, we remember the special role of Mary, the mother of Jesus.
You showed her the way through the Angel Gabriel and she responded obediently and joyfully.
Help us to be obedient and joyful in our preparation for Christmas.
Let darkness turn to light as we share the expectation of the season ahead.
We ask this through Jesus Christ, our Lord.
Amen

72 Almighty God,
we thank you for the special people who helped to prepare the way for Christmas.
For Moses and the patriarchs of ancient Israel; for the prophets who foretold the news of Christ's coming; for John the Baptist, who paved the way for Jesus; and for Mary who accepted your call to bring your Son into the world.
Come, Lord Jesus, for we await the arrival of the Light of the World.
We ask this through Jesus Christ, our Lord.
Amen

73 As we wait, we watch, we give thanks:
for your promises about to be fulfilled;
for your Son about to be with us, our Emmanuel.
May we show our respect and gratitude:
for Mary, who gave up a normal life
to be the mother of your Son;
for Joseph, who stayed loyal to the family;
for all who helped to bring your Son to a world in waiting.
We have so much to be thankful for
as the old covenant is transformed into the shock of the new.
Amen

74 Send your Holy Spirit to renew your Church.
May the spark be kindled in people and institutions
as people take stock of the meaning of this time of year,
in between parties and making merry.
Bring meaning to their lives
as your Son brought mercy to the world.
Like the shepherds in the fields,
may we stay alert to events unfolding.
Create in us a realisation
that there is something greater to comprehend,
a reality that surpasses our imagination.
Amen

75 We pray, Lord, that we can always be alert to your call,
ready to account for our lives,
ready to acknowledge you as Saviour,
ready to go wherever you need us to be.
Meanwhile, we ask that you prepare us
in our spiritual growth and development,
through the grace and fellowship of your Son,
whose love knows no bounds,
whose light shines out in every generation.
Amen

76 Send your blessings on the Church, we pray.
Give to church leaders a sense of destiny,
to guard and guide the ways of the faithful,
to encourage all those of religious faith,
and to challenge those who do not have a belief system.
This Advent, may our church prepare and prompt us in our own faith journey, so that our hearts may be lifted up
and our mission clarified for all in our church community.
Amen

77 God of righteousness,
show us your ways and teach us your paths,
and may the moon and the stars add to your glory,
even as they signal great change.
We give thanks for the promises to be fulfilled;

for the prophets in their vision and wisdom;
and for the days to come in our Advent journey.
May we look for the signs and search in our hearts
so that change and hope can go hand in hand,
sealing your love for us and our trust in you.
Amen

Christmas

78 As we recall the star that shone out above Bethlehem,
we thank you for the gift of your Son, the light of the world.
Let us join with people down the ages who have celebrated
this event and rejoice.
Amen

79 We pray for the Church worldwide at this special time,
remembering the places where worship is difficult or dangerous;
the places where worship is joyful but food is scarce;
and the places where the festive season
is mixed with worries about the future.
May your Son's birth bring hope to all communities
and may your Church be strengthened in all its work
to make you better known.
Amen

80 We rejoice at this Christmas season.
May fellowship and friendship
take the place of competitiveness and greed,
generosity replace selfishness.
Help us to remember the welcome given by the shepherds
as we bring your Son
into our hearts and into our lives once again.
Amen

81 Let this festive season bring hope to our world,
as we recall the timeless story of the first Christmas.
May we recapture the spirit of wonder
and rekindle in us the joy of the angels

that heralded your Son's arrival amongst us,
the promise of our salvation.
Amen

82 May the star that brought the wise men from the East
spread its light through the ages and attract us still.
Let us take inspiration from the Magi in their journey of faith,
using their knowledge to learn more and know you better.
Create in us that wonder and the humility that goes with it,
we pray.
Amen

83 God of new beginnings,
we rejoice with the angels
at the birth of your Son.
May we share the gift of hope
that this day brings for humankind.
Give us focus and friendship
so that real peace, your peace,
can break out – and be sustained.
As we watch and shepherds gather,
may the star of Bethlehem
shine brightly in our lives.
Amen

84 Almighty God,
we ask for your blessings
and offer you our thanks,
as Christmas once again enters our lives and hearts.
May the birth of your Son
bring gladness and neighbourliness,
even where there is hardship and hurt.
May our actions and thoughts
reflect the generosity of the gift of your Son, Jesus Christ,
to a world in need of your love.
Amen

85 Loving and faithful God,
you have entrusted your Son
to a world that rejected you,
giving humankind a second chance.
At this festive season, help us to seize the time
to give a second chance
to family relationships;
to help for neighbours;
to global awareness;
and above all, Lord,
to our relationship with you,
through our Emmanuel,
born this day.
Amen

86 God of hope,
lead us to your Son,
as we remember his birth.
Lead us to better ways,
as we follow his ways.
Lead us to watch and worship,
as the shepherds show us.
Lead us to celebrate in song,
as we join the music of the angels.
May the lasting legacy of that first Christmas
be that we put you first,
not just once a year, but for all time,
as your Son did.
Amen

87 Heavenly Father,
we thank you for all the wonderful things that happen at Christmas; the gifts that we give each other, the love that is shown for those in need.
But, above all, Lord, as the star shone out above Bethlehem on that first Christmas, we thank you for the gift of your Son, the Light of the World.
As Christmas comes, let us join with people down the ages who have celebrated this event and rejoice.
We thank you, Lord.
Amen

88 Heavenly Father,
make this Christmas special for all here today.
Even if we are unable to give presents, help us to give greetings; even if we do not receive what we want, help us to let people know that we are grateful that they thought of us. Help us to remember what it was like in that stable in Bethlehem, where the baby Jesus spent his first days with Mary, Joseph and the animals gathered round, shepherds assembled outside and the bright star showing the way to this place, your Son's first home.
We ask this in Jesus' name.
Amen

Epiphany

89 Lord of signs and symbols,
as the star beckoned Magi from distant lands,
so are we drawn by the birth of your Son,
over time as well as space.
Help us in our own age to go the extra mile,
to learn your ways and witness to your truth.
As we gather round the crib,
in church or in our imagination,
may we feel the anticipation of all around,
the humble and mighty,
brought together in wonder,
held together with hope,
as we are today.
Amen

90 Gracious God,
the gift of your Son was heralded by angels
and marked by the star that drew the Magi.
But we thank you that it was the shepherds
who were the first witnesses and the early evangelists,
as the word was spread about the holy birth.
Give us the vision to be there now,
in the outhouse amongst the animals,

Mary with the child and Joseph standing by.
As our Christmas gifts lose their shine,
may your gift to us grow in importance,
shaping our lives and pointing us to a bright future with you,
ever loving Lord.
Amen

91 Great shepherd of the sheep,
the birth of your Son changed everything,
and changes us still.
May we carry forward into the New Year
our hopes and your expectations,
the goodwill of Christmas,
the mended relationships,
and the spirit of giving and receiving.
But help us also, Lord,
to forgive any harsh words,
to get over disappointments,
and to renew the spirit of love,
in response to the great gift
of your Son, our Saviour, Jesus Christ.
Amen

92 God of all ages and all time,
create in us the wonder felt by the Magi
as they travelled far in faith and hope.
Send your Holy Spirit to awaken in us
the surprise of the shepherds,
the acceptance of Joseph,
the joy of the angels,
the love of Mary,
and the realisation that all things are made new,
in our relationship with you
and in the tender mercy of your grace,
which oversees your creation
and fills our lives
if we are open to your love.
Amen

93 Almighty God,
as wise men came travelling, we pray for travellers at this time of year, joining or leaving family and friends.
Help us to follow the wise men's example to make special efforts to reach out to things that are important, to go the extra mile to do the right thing.
Let us share the special times of Epiphany by honouring the presence of your Son in our lives, just as the wise men honoured the arrival of Jesus in their world
so many years ago.
We ask this through Jesus Christ, our Lord.
Amen

94 Almighty God,
just as the star brought the Magi to Bethlehem, create in us the desire
– to travel far to find the truth
– to bring gifts without expecting any in return
– to be open to wonder at your marvellous creation
– to hold on to the power of the Christian story in our daily lives.
Bring us, Lord, closer to you, as your Son's birth brought the wise men to Bethlehem.
We ask this through Jesus Christ, our Lord.
Amen

The Baptism of Christ

95 We ask, Lord,
that the gentleness and justice foreshadowed by Isaiah, and fulfilled in Jesus, are baptised afresh in us today. May the dove of the Holy Spirit come down on us,
as it did for Jesus,
and may we know the power of hope witnessed by John that day.
Amen

96 As we celebrate the baptism of Christ,
we give thanks for both the light of creation
and the light of the world, your Son, Jesus Christ.
Let the waters of the deep and the waters of the Jordan
be touched by your new creation.
And may the Holy Spirit bless the transformation John heralded and Jesus completed.
Amen

97 May our Church be baptised afresh in commitment
and transforming love when new Christenings take place.
Let our faith in Christ be renewed
and our efforts to nurture the faith of new Christians be redoubled.
And may those who lead our worship and ministry
do so in the grounding of your love and inspired by your Holy Spirit.
Amen

98 Lord, you have called us each by name to follow you.
When your Son was baptised by John in the Jordan
you met us and began to bring us home.
Let the Holy Spirit be always close to us and guard us
from the fear of stumbling in our faith.
Strengthen and renew us through the example of the apostles and the love of your Son.
Amen

99 We pray for the leaders of our churches
and the discipleship of the laity.
Wherever your name is acknowledged, in church and school, house and workplace, bring the spirit of mission and strength of purpose shown by your apostles.
And may we always draw inspiration from the humility of John and the servanthood of Christ
as your Church seeks to meet the challenges ahead.
Amen

The Presentation of Christ

100 God of power and might,
we give thanks that you have bridged the gap
between us and you through your Son.
Let us rejoice at the coming of the Light
to lighten our path and to glorify your name.
May we respond as the congregation in the Temple did
when Christ was presented
and Simeon and Anna announced the significance of that event. Let us also remember the mixed emotions of Mary
as she hears what will unfold.
Amen

101 God of great expectations,
lead your Church in your ways,
ready to respond to the unexpected,
able to guide your people into the way of peace,
prepared to challenge us to deepen our faith,
and inspired to bring the faith to those currently without belief. Make your mission our purpose.
Amen

Ash Wednesday

102 Heavenly Father,
you have seen the transgressions that we have committed,
the ways we have fallen short
in our behaviour and attitudes.
We seek your forgiveness,
knowing that your Son has redeemed
our sins through his sacrifice.
Strengthen us in our penitence and resolve
never to let you down.
During this Lenten season help us
to discipline ourselves to remain steadfast in faith,
learn new things and set our face
against returning to sinful ways.
Amen

103 May your Church lead by example in humility, service
and a right resolve to remain true to your ways.
Let the mission of our church be to prepare us
for the wonder of Easter by Bible study,
explanation of the Scriptures, prayers,
supplication and fasting.
Make us take on new responsibilities
as we let go of meaningless tasks,
and appreciate what we love by giving up
the things we really like.
Amen

Lent

104 Breathe on me, breath of life!
May your Spirit bring assurance of new life
and the hope of your kingdom.
Let the power of your vision, expressed through your Son,
transform our lives as it will transform our death.
Help us to understand all that you are giving to us, as we
follow the path of suffering of Jesus,
alongside Mary and John,
even to the foot of the cross.
Amen

105 Give to your Church, this Passiontide,
the will and the means to make a difference in people's lives
to show a glimpse of eternity in the joy of Easter.
But may the Church also share the nature of your Son's
suffering and hard-won victory over death.
Yours is not the easy path, but it is the right one, Lord,
for the world, for us, and for our relationship with you.
Amen

106 As we walk with your Son in his trials and passion,
may we be more observant of the world around us,
where there is suffering and hardship, pain and sacrifice.
We pray especially for the people of . . .

Deepen our commitment, Lord,
to our neighbours throughout the world
and let their challenges be our responsibility too.
Amen

107 Refreshing and renewing Lord,
you have led us through difficulties
and temptations and looked after us.
May we appreciate the benefits
you have brought us and the greatest gift
that you could ever give, your Son,
to live among us and die for us.
Bring us back into a right relationship with you, Lord,
in the knowledge that you never give up on us,
even if we have sometimes neglected you.
This Lent, deepen our faith and strengthen
our understanding of your Son's teaching
so that our trust in his witness to your love for us may grow.
Amen

108 Forgiving Lord,
may our Lenten journey bring us close to you
as we discipline ourselves
in study and in our daily lives,
taking new things on if we give things up
and opening our minds to new insights along the way.
Send us out in persistence and faith
to demonstrate the care and concern
your Son showed us, in his life and death.
It is the least that we can do
to show our gratitude
to the one who saved us
and suffered for us,
your Son, Jesus Christ.
Amen

109 Heavenly Father,
at this time we offer you our persistence and praise,
through fasting and giving up,
but also through studying and taking on.
May what we learn renew our hope
and bring us closer to your purpose.
As we seek to follow your Son's example,
in prayer, in social action, in selfless love,
give us strength to withstand the pressures of society,
which can draw us away,
as our discipline slips
and our faith falters.
Empower us with your Spirit,
equip us in your service.
Amen

110 Almighty God,
bring to us new insights this Lent,
so that in our worship and daily practice
we grow closer to you.
Let us for once put aside selfishness
And let your Son's selflessness draw us to him.
In learning what we miss
may we also learn what we really need,
but also what others around require,
neighbours, friends, and families,
as well as our neighbours across the world,
part of your family of humankind,
all made in your image.
Grant us the gift of peace
in the midst of the world's busyness.
Amen

111 Lord God,
may we be tested in the wilderness,
as your Son was.
May we find ourselves alone with you,
as your Son was.
May we learn to be connected with you,

as your Son was.
But, in this Lenten period,
as we approach the events of Holy Week,
let us give thanks that we are spared
the consequences of our past sins
through the forgiveness and salvation
taught and acted out
in your Son's ministry and suffering,
leading to the sacrifice of the crucifixion
and his glorious resurrection.
For all this, we thank and glorify you,
gracious God.
Amen

Mothering Sunday

112 We pray for mothers everywhere and for the gift of mothering,
which is shared amongst us all.
On this day, let us celebrate with you, Lord,
the joy and the pain experienced by mothers.
We are all sons or daughters and owe our lives and upbringing
to those who brought us into the world, as part of your
creation. May the love that your Son showed his mother Mary
shine in our lives too.
And may our duty of care to our mothers be transfused
with love, affection and gratitude.
Amen

113 May the Mother Church in which we have grown in faith
be blessed with the care and affection we show to our parents.
May authority be mixed with nurture
and teaching mixed with learning
so that we can become mature Christians in your presence,
Lord.
Help us shape the environment in which we worship
so that our lives can show the benefits of a growing
spirituality, walking closely with our God.
Amen

Palm Sunday

114 Hosanna to the King of kings!
Lord, we give thanks that your Son humbled himself on the cross, yet was exalted in his resurrection.
Your word was fulfilled, through his ordeal and our salvation.
But let us understand and feel the great suffering in this sacrifice, the tears shed, the pain experienced,
the abandonment felt.
May we who hear this story feel stronger for it
and more steadfast in our faith.
Amen

115 As the processions in and around our churches show to the world that the Easter story lives and that Jesus' suffering was not in vain,
may that hope spread out into communities across the land.
Give confidence to your Church in its outreach
and in its capacity to draw people in.
Let young and old alike hear this story
and share in the pain and the joy.
Amen

116 As the world looked on at your Son in his journey to the cross,
so may the world today know the extent of your love.
Give us all a glimpse of that sacrifice,
a taste of the degradation of the cross,
an idea of your generosity in the face of rejection.
Let the world know the power of redemption and be grateful.
And where there is oppression today, Lord,
bring your hope to the downtrodden,
remembering especially at this time . . .
Amen

117 God our Father, who understands suffering and loss,
help us to appreciate the enormity of your generosity
in sending your Son to minister to us
and bring us back from the brink.
As we cry 'Hosanna' and join the crowds in strewing the path

with palms, we look ahead to the crown of thorns awaiting him. May we recognise the glory to come in the way of the cross. Give us the strength to survive our own moments
of doubt and testing,
of challenge and pain,
knowing that we can never suffer as he suffered.
Amen

118 Let your Church 'do justice, love kindness and walk humbly' with you, our God.
As we approach the glory and joy of Easter,
we pray for the state of the Church,
so that your word can be spread
and your love can be known more widely.
Nurture and challenge our faith, Lord,
at this time in the church year
when we walk with your Son and watch with his mother,
knowing the glorious outcome,
but recognising the pain of the cross.
Amen

119 Lord, we have all denied you,
knowingly or unwittingly, as Peter did.
We give thanks for your Son's choice of ordinary people
as apostles and disciples,
so that we may all identify with them in our failings
as well as seek to emulate them
in the way we share the Christian story.
As we benefit from the forgiveness
and redemptive power of your Son,
so may we acknowledge the way to encourage and empower
the growth of faith, whatever the imperfections
and human frailties within us and around us.
Amen

120 We pray for archbishops, bishops, and priests
throughout your Church,
as they rededicate their ministry
and reach out through baptism to a receptive world.
Bring to congregations an appetite for learning
and a desire to share ministry and mission.
Help us to seek new ways to sustain our church
in ministering to the needs of the community.
Amen

121 May we reach out to the needs of the world
in all we say and do as Christians.
Just as the centurion at the cross knew that Jesus was innocent,
so there are many who look to the Church for values and
meaning, in the midst of anger and suffering.
Deepen our commitment to God in the world.
Help us to see you in the darkness of conflict
as well as in the beauty of creation,
so that we can share your hope with those who seek it.
We pray especially for the people of . . .
Amen

Holy Week and Easter

122 Heavenly Father,
during this Holy Week, when so much is lost and so much
is gained, we remember Jesus' entry into Jerusalem, his
betrayal, his suffering, and his crucifixion.
We think of the disciple who claimed not to know him,
the mother who went to the foot of the cross with him
and the Roman centurion who knew this was the Son of God.
Help us to think every day of this week about the feelings
of Jesus and all those around him.
We ask this in Jesus' name.
Amen

123 Almighty God,
we pray that as we engage with the unfolding of Holy Week
we enter into the characters of those who play a crucial role,
from Pilate to Peter, from bystander to Barabbas,
from Mark to Mary.
Let us breathe in the tension of betrayal
and the sense of isolation of Jesus, your Son,
before experiencing the new dawn of Easter.
Amen

124 Heavenly Father,
at Easter time we pray for new life to come out of
the suffering of Jesus on the cross.
We share the joy of the resurrection on Easter Sunday,
just as we shared the sorrow and suffering of Holy Week.
Give us the hope to look forward knowing that our sins
have been forgiven.
Help us to understand that out of the agony of Good Friday
has come the joy of Easter.
Alleluia, Christ is risen!
Amen

125 Heavenly Father,
may we use this time to look back and look forward:
seeing the culmination of Jesus' earthly ministry
through the eyes of the ordinary people who witnessed
the events of that special week;
the hope, the bewilderment, the mystery,
the agony, the despair and the triumph.
Take us through the mix of emotions
which preceded the alleluias of the resurrection.
Amen

Maundy Thursday

126 Lord, we pray that in our service to others
we can show the humility and the loving service
that your Son demonstrated to the disciples

in the act of washing their feet.
We give thanks that he has also shared the bread and the wine of the last supper in remembrance of him.
Your Son taught us a new commandment
to love one another as he loved us.
May our service to each other be modelled on our service to you and may our hope be in him who has saved us from our selfishness and pride.
Amen

127 We rejoice that our Teacher and Lord has stooped
to wash the feet of those he led and served.
Let our church leaders follow his example in the humble ministry and exemplary leadership they show in carrying out their duties.
Let prayer and worship underpin all that bishops and priests do in your name.
Create in churches across the world a focus and a priority on an event which makes all things new.
Amen

Good Friday

Prayers in a community setting before recreating the walk with the cross to Golgotha.

128 God of love and sacrifice,
we offer you our thanks and praise
on this day, Good Friday,
in this town of . . . ,
for all your goodness and loving kindness.
As we prepare to make our way to the hills above us,
we recall and retrace
the way of the cross that your Son followed
in obedience to you.
Thank you, Lord, thank you, Jesus.
Amen

129 God of grace,
enfold . . . with your love,
as Churches Together in . . . seek to enfold this town
with our prayers.
Help us to love our neighbours;
to cherish our community
and to walk humbly with you, our God.
For Jesus' Christ sake.
Amen

130 Caring God,
watch over all the helping agencies and volunteers
throughout . . .
As we gather we ask for your blessings
on their work of help and hope
on behalf of the least, the lost and the lonely,
the hungry, the homeless and those without hope.
We give our heartfelt thanks
that you have rescued us from our misdoings and
shortcomings through the example and sacrifice of your
Son, Jesus Christ.
Amen

131 Almighty and ever-living God,
on this Good Friday may we:
recommit ourselves to you;
reconnect ourselves to our community;
and renew our confidence in Christ.
Pour your blessings on . . . ,
expect great things from us,
as we wonder at what you have done for us.
May your Holy Spirit
empower and equip us to do your will,
to your praise and glory,
in Jesus' name.
Amen

132 All we, like sheep, have gone astray.
We have been rescued, Lord, by the lamb sacrificed for us.
On this day of terrible mystery and darkness,
we look for signs of hope.
We marvel at the pity of your Son for his mother and brother,
at the acceptance of his destiny and the fulfilment of his mission.
We are deeply grateful, Father God, that you enabled
Jesus to go through his ordeal without your intervention
and shared the grief of those around him.
Amen

133 This is a time of challenge for your Church, loving God.
We give thanks that you have graciously steered it through to this day,
despite the twin challenges of the world outside
and quarrels within.
Bring us together at the foot of the cross in common purpose,
so that we may share in the fruits of the salvation
of the resurrection.
Amen

Easter Eve

134 Lord of new beginnings,
we yearn for sight of your Son, as we watch and wait,
hoping against hope that the grave cannot hold him.
We ask that our sorrow can turn to joy,
so that his destiny is fulfilled and your purpose is achieved.
Let us take nothing for granted
in acknowledging the bounty of your love, through your Son.
Amen

135 Your Church waits and prays, Lord.
May we be led into truth and righteousness
through the example of your Son.
No sacrifice we make can equate to his sacrifice for us.
As we await the promised resurrection,

help us reflect on his self-giving love
and commit ourselves to show that love in our lives,
to accept such love from others, and to renew our vow
to resist evil and turn to Christ.
Amen

136 As the world seeks to close the tomb and largely turns its back,
we pray that eyes refocus on the events unfolding
in a place which is never out of the spotlight.
Open hearts and minds, Lord,
in the sure and certain knowledge
that all things are possible under God.
Deepen our resolve to look for hope in corners of the world
that are suffering now, including . . .
Amen

Easter

137 God of glory,
we sing your praises, this special day.
Halleluiah, risen Lord!
Halleluiah, love triumphant!
Halleluiah, Redeemer, Saviour!
May the joy that we feel
create a wave of peace and celebration
which washes away doubt and fear
and brings hope and reconciliation
to a broken world
and a new beginning for humankind.
Amen

138 Father of all,
we give thanks that your promise has been fulfilled,
that your Son has broken through the barrier of death,
for us and for all humankind,
having taken on the burden of our sins:
all have been washed away in the blood of Good Friday
and now the transformation is accomplished,
through the resurrection of that first Easter morning.

May prophet and priest, president and monarch,
rejoice with us and all the saints,
that we are held in your hands,
shielded and redeemed by your Son,
our Saviour, Jesus Christ.
Amen

139 God of promise and purpose,
we thank you that your Son
risked all for us, in his life and death.
We rejoice with you at his rising to new life,
just as you promised for those
who keep firm in faith and true to you.
May we seek to extend your kingdom,
in every way we can,
in church and in community,
in witness and in mission,
so that the good news continues
from generation to generation
and extends to every neighbourhood,
near and far, accessible and remote.
Inspire us daily as we have been inspired today,
Alleluia, alleluia.
Amen

140 Heavenly Father,
say it's so,
that Christ is risen.
Make it so,
that we are saved.
Let it be,
that you are with us.
Help us see
that death is conquered.
As we start afresh, in hope and trust,
lead us by the example of your Son
and the guidance of your Holy Spirit,
so that we can accomplish
all that your risen Son would wish.
Amen

141 Alleluia!
We give thanks for this new dawn in the story of humanity,
your creation, Lord.
You have brought back your only Son from the death
inflicted by those he came to save.
As we rejoice in his resurrection, let us commit ourselves
anew to see your hand in the hope that radiates out
from this great event.
Like Mary in the garden, may we glory in the ordinary,
glimpse eternity in a small flower.
Great is the day that you have made, Lord, for us all.
Amen

142 We ask for your blessings on your Church
as it keeps the flame of faith burning in our hearts.
Refresh and restore our relationship with you, Lord,
through the nurture and challenge of our church leaders.
Make them reach out to you and to us in all their ministry:
in worship, in pastoring, in mentoring.
Empower them in your Spirit, as the ripples of this day
once again spread your word abroad.
Amen

143 God of mystery and liberation,
your Son has broken free from the tomb
and has rescued us from the burden of sin.
We give thanks that this momentous happening
quietly and quickly gained currency
and still does so today across the world.
We ask that the new life of the resurrection
becomes our guide and our shield in all we do.
Bring us constantly back to the miracle of the open tomb
whenever we doubt or when we stray into backwaters of belief.
Today we have good news to proclaim, so let us be glad.
Amen

144 We thank you, Lord, for the ministry of your Church
in sharing your word and witnessing to your love.
Help us all to strengthen the bond
between church and community,
between you and us, between past and future.

Deepen our understanding of the old and new testaments,
the old and new covenants.
Make our church a real learning community
with your Son, the risen Saviour, as our teacher and role model.
Amen

145 As we celebrate the feast of Easter,
after the penitence of Lent and the sorrow of Good Friday,
let us not forget the parts of the world where sorrow and hardship are the norm, especially . . . and where natural forces have caused destruction, remembering . . .
May the joy of Easter break through poverty and distress
and may Christians everywhere always seek justice,
alongside meeting the urgent needs of day-to-day living
amongst neighbours near and far.
Amen

146 Lord, we rejoice and are glad on this day of days,
when you have created a new heaven and a new earth.
Like Peter and Mark and Mary Magdalene,
we wonder at the marvel of your Son's resurrection,
even though none of us should be surprised.
You have fulfilled your promise,
made through the prophets and heralded by your Son.
May we keep our side of the bargain
and live up to the trust given to us to keep your ways,
even in the face of evil and indifference.
Thank you for the hope your Son has brought to us.
Amen

147 May the Church shape our faith
so that we are constant and eager learners,
ardent and gracious sharers.
Equip us, we ask, Lord, to live up to the standards your Son has set in showing self-giving love, pastoral concern for the world beyond our comfort zone,
and a special place in our hearts for a desire to know you better, merciful God.
Amen

148 Help us to serve you in the world, Lord,
in the dark places as well as the open spaces,
amongst those we may not like as well as those we love.
You command that we love our neighbour as ourselves.
On this Easter Day, celebrated by rich and poor alike,
on every continent and in every land,
make clear to us how we should bring assistance
and genuine compassion
to troubled people and places, remembering especially . . .
Amen

Ascension

149 Faithful God,
at this Ascensiontide we give thanks
for entrusting us with your Son,
for never giving up on us,
even though we have often ignored you.
As your Son ascends and your Spirit descends,
we ask for your blessings on our Church,
which you have empowered and equipped
to sustain the faith,
to nurture disciples,
and to continue the task
begun, inspired and continued
through the risen Christ.
Amen

150 Blessed Trinity,
reunited and indivisible,
strengthen us in our daily round,
our common tasks, our mission duties.
In church and in prayer,
restore and renew our trust in you,
so that we can extend your kingdom,
in the sure knowledge of your love and oversight.
You have transformed us through the cross,
trusted us in the Ascension,

equipped as through the Spirit.
Accompany us in our journey
as we explore our path back to you,
safe at last.
Amen

151 Loving Lord,
let us always give thanks for gifts
that help us to grow in faith.
Just as you sent your Son
on a mercy mission to save fallen humankind,
so your Son put in place a stairway to heaven
through the perseverance of your disciples
in setting up your Church
so that where your Son has gone
we may follow.
By your grace and our faith,
may we join him on that stairway,
through your Son, Jesus Christ.
Amen

152 Eternal Father,
your Son restored, redeemed and brought us back to you.
As he ascends to your right hand,
we rejoice at the scale of his intervention,
at the sheer transforming power of his love,
and your great goodness in sending him to us.
We are no longer on our own,
as we have the Holy Spirit, the Comforter,
to guide our path and order our ways.
May we be faithful and fruitful
in discharging our duties through your Church,
dear Lord and father of humankind.
Amen

Pentecost

153 Almighty God,
fill us with your Holy Spirit,
just as your disciples experienced
in the rush of wind at Pentecost,
enabling, empowering, enthusing,
giving fresh insights and new understanding.
May we call on your Spirit,
in good times and bad, in sleep and rest,
and may we share with confidence
our faith, our hope, your truth.
Breathe on me, breath of God,
and set my spirit free.
Amen

154 Transforming God,
bring us the gift of communication,
just as you set the disciples free
to speak in different tongues
and be understood by all.
May we always seek to engage with people
in ways and in language
both appropriate and sensitive.
Never let us withhold understanding of your word,
through teaching, metaphor or example
which fails to be true to you
and falls short of the clarity
your Son would wish.
Amen

155 God of our Church,
let us welcome the breath of fresh air of your Holy Spirit,
in our worship,
in our hearts,
in our relationships,
in our parish life.
May the flames of faith be fanned
as we eagerly listen to your word.
And may we be touched

by the love you have shown
in sending the Holy Spirit as Comforter,
through Jesus Christ, our Lord.
Amen

156 God of hope and help,
we are doubly blessed
through the coming of the Holy Spirit
to guide us on the path your Son showed us.
May we, in church and at home,
be constantly refreshed and truly transformed
when we turn to you,
not just for ourselves,
but for friends and family,
and for people across the world,
So that we can be better instruments of your peace
and good communicators, in word and deed,
of your kingdom.
Amen

157 Lord of great blessings,
bring us into a right relationship with you
as we see the fruits of the Holy Spirit
in our lives and in our communities.
Let loose the wind of truth to work its wonder
by blowing where it will
and providing us with the power and the courage
to give voice to your will in all we do,
to your greater glory.
Amen

158 God of great adventure,
as we celebrate the gift of the Holy Spirit
let us experience in our worship
some of the wonder the disciples felt in their lives.
As we gaze upon you,
may we experience your grace
and, as we sing your praises,
may we know the fellowship
that comes with shared faith and certain hope.
Amen

159 Bring us the benefit of your Holy Spirit
as we seek to renew and refresh our spiritual lives,
to do justice to the sheer extravagance of your love for us.
May our lives be turned around and upside down,
encouraging us to step out onto the high wire of faith,
knowing you are our safety net,
our plumb-line and lodestar,
an ever present help in time of trouble
and a sure guide along the way.
Amen

160 God of speech and sign,
give to us the zeal of the disciples
and their ability to share our faith with others.
May we be open to the Holy Spirit
to show us new ways of giving life to your Truth,
ever mindful of the need to communicate
with confidence and commitment
and a desire to do your will in all we attempt in Jesus' name.
Amen

161 Almighty God,
bring your Holy Spirit to work in our hearts.
Let the wind and the flames that the disciples felt renew our faith.
Help us to show the Holy Spirit in our lives that others may know your love and learn your way.
We ask this through Jesus Christ, our Lord.
Amen

162 Almighty God,
as we celebrate the receiving of the Holy Spirit by the disciples, we ask that we can know the Holy Spirit too.
If we cannot feel this wind in the same way as the disciples,
bring us the fruits of the Spirit in other ways.
If we cannot understand or communicate in many tongues,
help us to try to communicate God's love
in the best way we can.
May Pentecost show, in our lives, that we depend on Jesus
even though we do not see him, and feel his presence with

the help of the comforter, the Holy Spirit.
We ask this through Jesus Christ, our Lord.
Amen

163 God of promise and glory,
you raised your Son from the dead to redeem us
and now you receive him back to reign with you.
We give you thanks for the transformation of our lives
through the wonder of Easter,
as we look forward to the coming of the Holy Spirit to sustain us.
Grace us with your presence in our lives,
as real as when you stood with the disciples,
as ready to love as you loved them.
Help us to return your love through word and deed.
Amen

164 God of great promises,
you have been true to your Word
in sending us your Son and receiving him home.
We give you praise and thanks
for his ministry among us,
preparing and equipping us for our ministry
and sending us the Holy Spirit as our helper.
May we all feel your holy presence
as the Holy Spirit does his work
and we rise to the challenges you have set before us.
Amen

165 Let your Church ring out praise and celebration
of your Son's ascension,
in the confidence that your Holy Spirit refreshes and renews our faith and worship.
May the Church itself rise to the challenge of its task
in taking you to the ends of the earth,
glorifying your name in adoration.
Give the Church the power to transform lives
as your Son gave us the gift of hope
and the means to show this to others.
Amen

166 Heavenly Father,
may your Son's ascension
bring hope and glory to your Church,
so that your Holy Spirit restores us
in our mission and harmony,
raising our sights and widening our horizons
in making yo…ur love known.
Amen

167 Lord, you have given us the vision to dream dreams.
Now through the Holy Spirit may we show and share your gifts to all who will listen, look and learn.
Help us to support each other in the task of mission,
remembering your Son's instructions in sending out his disciples.
Breathe on us, gracious God,
the wind and the fire of your inspiration
so that we can be confident that you are with us
and in us when we face difficult challenges.
Amen

168 We pray that you may equip your Church,
this church, to do you justice and honour,
in worship and prayer, mission and pastoral care.
Let service to others be at the heart of our purpose,
as it was for your Son.
Strengthen us in our resolve to make a difference,
to bring understanding
and to trust your Holy Spirit to guide us.
Amen

169 Father of all,
we yearn for the Spirit of truth in our lives,
confident in the hope that you bring.
May the Holy Spirit blow away our doubt and our reticence
in matters of faith.
Help us to deepen our awareness of you, we ask, Lord,
by drawing on the experience and example of the disciples

who spread your word in the power of the Spirit
and in union with your Son.
Amen

170 We pray for the leaders of the Church
in their work of mission, ministry and management.
Give them wisdom in displaying their gifts and resources
so that people may see Jesus.
Let ecumenical work flourish so that there can be unity
in the diversity of churches proclaiming your word.
May it be your will and our task to encourage joint working,
as we all worship the one Lord,
Father, Son and Holy Spirit.
Amen

171 We thank you, O God, for the universality of your message
conveyed by the disciples through your Holy Spirit.
The sign of hope has been shown to us
through your Son's intervention in the world
and we rejoice at your presence in our lives today.
Guide us in our spiritual journeys, firm in the knowledge
that you will provide the means for us to find you
if we trust you as you have trusted us.
Amen

172 Help us to reflect on what the Holy Spirit brings to our church.
Is the flame alive in our hearts, in our words, in our worship?
May our spiritual leaders bring inspiration as well as humility
to the challenges that face your Church.
Give them the strength and the courage, Lord,
to carry on in the face of criticism and comment from all sides,
and may we support them through our prayers
and through our practical love.
Amen

Trinity Sunday

173 How great are your works and your achievements,
sovereign God, Father, Son and Holy Spirit.
We pray that the paths of justice and righteousness
can be followed by us, your children,
in response to your love for us.
Give us the chance to change, the will to do good,
and the commitment to be your witness, all the days of our lives.
And may we sometimes soar like eagles
as we wonder at your creation.
Amen

174 Heavenly Father,
you have shown us the spirit of truth through your Son
and, now, through the Holy Spirit.
Bestow on us, we pray,
the gift of discernment in seeking the right way forward
in the faith of Christ.
May your call steer our path into the right commitment,
knowing you are there to guard us and guide us in our choices.
Let joy accompany our search for the right way to honour you and love our God.
Amen

175 Exalted God, three in one,
we give thanks for the transformation of humanity that you have brought about through the intervention of your Son.
May the Holy Spirit continue his work among us
and equip us for the tasks ahead,
just as the disciples were empowered to do your will
throughout the known world.
Give us the grace, we pray, to acknowledge the important work
of those who have gone before – and be grateful.
Amen

Bible Sunday

176 O God of story and tradition,
we give thanks for the Bible which teaches us;
for the prophets, priests and kings who wrote it;
and for the central figure in the narrative we have inherited,
which is you, in the form of Father, Son and Holy Spirit.
Today we thank Nehemiah, Paul and Matthew
for the insights they have given us,
crossing over time and space to engage us today
in the common values and the shared lot of the people of God
through the ages.
Amen

177 May your Church and our church schools
ring out with the sound of your praises;
resound with the telling of stories from the Bible;
and bring interpretation and illumination from gospel and
epistle, psalm and revelation.
And may the sacred book of the Old Testament and the four
gospels be read and remembered, honoured and repeated,
from this generation to the next, from age to age.
Amen

178 Let us remember that the lands of the Bible
only seemed to extend to the known world.
Now that the rest of the planet has been revealed to us,
and the universe awaits,
may we marvel in wonder and praise
and commit ourselves to read with new eyes and listen afresh
to the greatest stories ever told, of prophets and preachers
and of your own dear Son, our Saviour.
Amen

179 God of truth,
keep our eyes firmly on the books of the Bible,
not on myth and magic, fantasy and hearsay.
And may all those Scriptures point to you,
through the wonderful story of your Son's coming,

foretold, described, and acted on,
from early days to latter days;
from here to eternity;
from you to us and then home to you.
Give us the wisdom to interpret the Bible correctly
and the joy of reading it regularly.
Amen

180 Grant to your Church the great gift of bringing the Bible alive,
revisiting and singing the revelation of your word,
and praying for your kingdom silently and in intercessions.
We thank you for the priests you have provided
and ask that others with a genuine vocation
are brought forward and tested
in order to secure that planning for succession
which your Son perfected and the disciples enacted.
Amen

181 Lord of Scripture and revelation,
we give thanks for the prophets and the scribes
who set forth your vision of the new covenant
for those who would listen and learn.
We marvel at the young Jesus
proclaiming your favour and the release of captives,
bringing us into a new heaven and a new earth,
heralded and then recorded as your holy word.
Amen

182 We pray that the hope and encouragement
we have been given in the Scriptures
may underpin and inform the way of your Church,
both the manner of its mission to the poor and oppressed
and the challenge to the faithful to be creative and fruitful
in the way we can translate into action
all the learning that comes from studying Scripture.
Amen

Dedication Festival

183 God of time and space,
we thank you for the holy places
where we can know you more deeply and see you more clearly.
May we always look beyond the beauty and the peace
to know your presence in our lives
so that wherever we go and whatever we do,
you are always with us, always in front of us, always in us.
Keep away the things which deflect us from you
and keep us focused on your will and purpose.
Amen

184 Your Church has provided refuge and holy ground
for our worship, prayer and praise.
Give all involved in our church
the sensitivity to know this,
the awareness to sustain it,
and the desire to develop it.
And may our churches everywhere
be a reminder of your reach beyond the building
and into the community,
an expression of your love for all humanity.
Amen

185 Lord of renewal,
may new and restored buildings resound with praise
and thanksgiving
as people gather to worship your name.
Let beautiful surroundings enhance our experience of you
and may they remind us of sacrifices made,
above all that of your Son.
Nothing that is worth doing is easily won
and we applaud the efforts of builders and stonemasons
which allow us to use holy space properly,
bringing us closer to you and you closer to us.
Amen

186 We ask for your blessings on your Church,
and especially in this building as holy ground and a place of worship.
May we appreciate all the signs and symbols of your presence
in our prayers and praise, in our contemplation and reflections.
In all our church activities,
let us draw on the inspiration of this place
to reach out into the community,
as our church reaches up to meet you.
Amen

187 O God, our rock and foundation,
may we honour and cherish the buildings
which provide a reminder of the bridge between heaven and earth,
represented by the cornerstone of our faith, your Son, our Saviour.
We know that all things come from you,
so let us give thanks in songs of praise
and prayer of quiet reflection, in this holy space,
offering all that we have and all that we are to your purpose.
Amen

188 We pray for your Church in all its diversity,
but with the unity of your Son at its still centre.
May our Church leaders be aware of the efforts and sacrifices of their predecessors
as well as discerning your will for the future.
We give thanks for the care and attention paid to the upkeep of our church buildings.
May even more effort go into the maintenance
and development of our faith
so that we can truly reflect the energy of the early Church
and honour the prayers of communities down the ages
that your kingdom can truly come,
in both this world and the next.
Amen

Harvest

189 Heavenly Father,
as the harvest is gathered in we praise you for all that is growing and picked and eaten at this time of year.
In thanking you, we also remember the hard work of the farmers who planted and fed and tended the crops, transported the food and made it all available to us.
We take this opportunity also, Lord, to pray for areas of the country and the wider world where crops have failed this year and where food is short.
May communities with plenty help those who have little.
We ask this in Jesus' name.
Amen

190 God of plenty,
we thank you for the fruits of the earth at this harvest time.
May we always remember the link between the food on our plate and the fields and farms around us.
Help us to choose and use our food wisely.
Bring food and water to the people who need them and restraint and generosity to the people who have more than enough.
We ask this in Jesus' name.
Amen

191 Lavish Lord,
you have provided for us in abundance,
so let us share with generosity and give thanks and praise with joy.
We know you love a cheerful giver
and would not wish us to show ingratitude.
Help us to sow the right seeds at the right time
and trust us to nurture growth right up to harvest.
Grant us your grace in this task, extravagant God.
Amen

192 We pray for your Church in every part of the land
and in every corner of the world.
May those in authority draw on your light and warmth;

on the refreshment of your Spirit;
and on the wisdom of those who have gone before;
so that green shoots can flourish in churches everywhere
and the fruits of the work of the Church
can bring forth new leaders and new, active Christians
to reflect your energy, your glory, your love.
Amen

193 You have given us resources aplenty
and the creativity to distribute them justly.
May our leaders and governments trade fairly, govern justly,
and take their cue from your Son's words and deeds.
Let the abundance of your love
extend to actions as well as material things,
encouraging freedom and liberty,
good works and just causes,
enabling rather than controlling others.
We pray especially for leaders in . . . at this time
and for a wiser approach to prevail.
Amen

194 God of overflowing generosity,
you taught us how to pray
through supplication, intercession
and thanksgiving made for everyone.
Grant us that enthusiasm for your creation
that we can communicate to others,
in order to help build our relationship with you, loving Lord,
as we rejoice in the harvest today.
Amen

195 We ask for your blessings on the universal Church.
Grant that in all our work in and for this church
we do not run the danger of building a church community
which serves us first and you next.
May we be forever grateful for the gifts and resources
you have granted us
and make us mindful of our need to pass on our knowledge
of how to apply them in every generation.

Raise up faithful and eager learners of your way
and help them to discern your will for them
so that vocations can be identified and nurtured
to the glory of your name and the benefit of your Church.
Amen

196 As we survey your creation, Lord,
may we wonder and learn:
wonder at the sheer beauty and infinite variety;
learn from the birds of the air
and the creatures of the earth
who live for the day, but adorn your world.
Grant us the means as well as the will
to conserve and safeguard the forest and the wilderness,
the flora and fauna, the fishes and farms,
remembering especially the current threat to . . .
and share the pain of suffering and the joy of recovery.
Amen

197 Bountiful God,
you gave us bread to eat and bread for life.
Grant us a good harvest and grateful hearts.
May we serve you with gladness
and follow your ways in humility.
As we recall the manna sent from heaven
to your people in the wilderness,
we rejoice at the provision you make
to sustain life in all its abundance.
Amen

198 We pray for your Church:
for the freedom and authority you have given it;
for the awareness it must have to be both courageous and sensitive;
for the tasks before us in discipleship;
for the brokenness that must be healed;
and for the leaders you discern – and we deserve.
Amen

199 We ask for your blessings on all who work on the land,
all who sow, all who tend, all who harvest.
We give thanks for the different skills and talents at work
which bring to our table the fruits of the earth.
We also pray for those who take risks
to bring us the season's riches of fish,
but may we hold back in our appetite for more,
so that species can flourish and grow up again.
We especially bring before you endangered stocks of . . .
and ask that agreement can be reached between people and nations
to honour your generosity.
Amen

Saints (general)

200 Holy Lord,
as we celebrate St . . .
we remember all the saints,
those who are special to us and our church,
those whose stories still inspire us today,
those unnamed saints whose unsung witness made a difference,
and those who are the saints of today, in your eyes, Lord.
Allow us our human role models,
who followed the example of your Son,
some even to death.
We thank you for their lives and their story, Lord.
Amen

201 Loving Lord,
in remembering our patron, St . . .
we honour *his/her* name and give thanks for *his/her* life.
May we learn from the witness and sacrifice of all the saints,
be inspired by their faithfulness,
and share their stories with others.
Give us the confidence which they had
to proclaim your name and keep your laws.

In a moment's silence, we bring before you
the saints of today who serve you
in ways which advance your kingdom,
. . .
Lord, uphold them in their mission.
Amen

202 Generous God,
you have poured your gifts on the saints through the ages.
Bring learning and purpose to our study of saints, day by day.
In this place, on this day, we give thanks for St . . .
May our lives be shaped by the legacy of this and all the saints,
not at the expense of your Son,
but to illuminate the path he trod,
the way, the truth, and the life he revealed
and the redemption he bought us,
in the lives of saints and martyrs.
Amen

203 Eternal God,
as we celebrate the saints in heaven
and the saints of the Christian Church,
so we acknowledge the sainthood of all believers.
May all those who profess your name
be mindful of the saints who have gone before.
And in a moment's silence
we recall those saints who have special meaning for us:
. . .
May we grow to be more like them
in our faith, our life, our hope.
Amen

204 God of saints and sainthood,
look on your people with compassion
and help us with models and examples
of the one true Way,
beacons of hope in troubled times.
May their commitment and passion

point us to the price your Son paid
to rid us of sin and the fear of death.
Amen

205 Lord of symbols and signs,
in our commemoration of saints,
let us not forget the saints of our time,
in lands near and far,
who have faced danger fair and square
and continued to proclaim the faith,
even in the face of threats of violence.
May we honour them, alongside the saints of old,
as brave disciples and witnesses
to your saving power.
Amen

206 Great God of truth,
you sent your Holy Spirit on your disciples
to strengthen and encourage them in their ministry.
As we celebrate the sainthood of all believers,
help us to pick out the saints in our lives,
those whose Christian example has made a difference
through selfless actions and sacrificial ministry.
Amen

207 Surprising Lord,
bring us a glimpse of inspiring people
who have shaped the Christian faith
– and continue to do so.
Let the flame of faith you have kindled grow bright,
even in the face of near total eclipse.
May we always see the bright corona
of your Son's love shine through,
however and whenever it seems temporarily obscured.
Amen

All Saints' Day (1 November)

208 God of the new heaven and earth,
we give thanks for all the saints
who have foretold your Son's coming or who have kept the faith
in the face of persecution and doubt.
Blessed are all those who keep the flame alive,
day after day, without fear or favour,
humble and merciful, meek and dutiful.
Whatever the nature of their righteousness and sacrifice,
they have brought us all closer to you, our God.
Amen

209 We pray for your Church and those who sustain it,
over the centuries and across the globe.
Let every nation and every culture
have saints who reflect your universal glory,
as well as the origin of the Church in each land.
We marvel at the way in which our predecessors
marked the deeds of the early saints
and rejoice that we can pray with and through the saints,
seeking the amendment of life and the promise of the life to come.
Amen

210 Almighty God,
today we remember all the saints who have shaped the Christian story.
Those who died for their faith, remembering especially . . . ;
those who through their lives and works ensured the foundation of our faith, remembering in particular Mary the mother of Jesus; and those from our own communities and families who have made a difference as Christian people.
We thank you for all those saints who are now at peace with you.
Amen

211 Almighty God,
you know that we each have our special saints whose lives and works mean a lot to us.
In a moment of silence we remember them now.
Thank you, Lord, for who they were, what they did and what they still mean to us today.
Amen

All Souls' Day (2 November)

212 Heavenly Father,
on the day of All Souls we remember those who have died, and especially those who are known to us and our families and who are now at peace with you.
Create in us not the fear of death, but grateful thanks for their lives.
Keep away the doubts and dangers of those who are disrespectful of the dead.
Show your love to those who have recently lost someone close to them.
We ask this in Jesus' name.
Amen

213 Heavenly Father,
help us to remember and celebrate the lives of those who have died.
You have shown us through your Son's death and resurrection at Easter that death is not the end, but a new beginning.
In this world, let us not forget all who went before us,
the famous and the little known,
those who died young and those who lived long.
We know you loved them all, Lord, and still love them now.
May we remember and give thanks, may we never forget.
We ask this in Jesus' name.
Amen

Christ the King

214 O God,
whose Son came to reign in majesty,
we give thanks for his justice and mercy
as our shepherd and our teacher.
May we continue to be responsive to his call
when he seeks to protect us and when he challenges us.
When we need help in deciding what to do,
let us always take his example as our model
and seek clues to our behaviour from his parables.
More than anything, let us be unstinting in our praise
and thanksgiving.
Amen

215 We pray for your Church
and especially for all priests and deacons.
May they, and we, honour the vision of your Son and his
disciples
in founding the Church
which has developed into our Church today.
Let us rejoice in the diversity of the churches
rather than the differences between them,
as we pray for the unity which your Son would want
and which would help us to make a bigger impact
in our mission to the world.
Grant wisdom to our archbishops and bishops
as they bring your word and your Son's deeds
to the attention of governments and royalty.
Amen

216 God of power and might,
your Son came to be amongst us as saviour and king,
even though his kingdom was unknown to Pilate
who struggled to understand the source of his power.
May we understand what Pilate failed to comprehend
as we honour his lordship over all that is important
and try to obey his command and example.
Grant us insight and faith to follow his way
and not be deflected in carrying out his purpose.
Amen

217 Bring down your Holy Spirit on your Son's Church,
to equip it with the faithful witness
shown by your Son in his ministry.
May priests be inspired in word and deed
and may our own church reverberate with songs of praise
to the King of kings and Lord of lords.
Let all your people know from us
the extent of your love for them.
Amen

218 God our Father,
you are the first and the last in all creation.
We give thanks for the privilege of your Son's presence with us
to save us from our sins by repentance and forgiveness,
to be sacrificed and resurrected for our benefit
and to be the architect of your Church, which continues to serve you
through the efforts of your faithful servants, saints and martyrs.
May we worship and adore you
as we hear and heed the words of your Son.
Let his reign be for everlasting
and our love for him unswerving.
Amen

219 As guardian of your Church and keeper of your word,
may clergy, and all who minister,
be steadfast and true in their life and ministry
as they seek to maintain the effectiveness and influence
of the Church's mission to extend your kingdom
in home and family, government and community.
Amen

PRINCIPAL SAINTS

(The feast days given here are those which appear in Common Worship. For more saints see 'Prayers for Saints', details of which appear in the bibliography at the end of this book. In all cases the date in brackets is the date of death, as far as is known.)

220 **2 January**
Basil the Great (379) and Gregory of Nazianzus (389), bishops and teachers of the faith

We look back with awe and gratitude to the early fathers, Basil and Gregory, friends and defenders of the divinity of your Son. We are blessed that Gregory's prayer and oratory combined with Basil's commitment and will to distil and establish the Creed we say today, by which we express the faith we are happy to call Christianity.
Amen

221 **13 January**
Hilary, Bishop of Poitiers and teacher (367)

Father, Son and Holy Spirit, who blessed your defender and advocate, Hilary, for his staunch and persistent loyalty to the true faith, may we have the same determination in the face of threats to the core Christian beliefs. Despite exile and decrees against him, we celebrate the triumph of 'the Athanasius of the West' as we remember him today and in the name given to the university term starting at this time.
Amen

222 **17 January**
Antony of Egypt, hermit and abbot (356)

God of space and silence, we give thanks for the desert father, Antony, and his example of selfless and possessionless living. May his life as a hermit, fleeing from the world yet praying for this world, help us to restore a proper balance between doing and being, between fellowship and solitude.
Amen

223 **21 January**
Agnes, child martyr at Rome (304)

Merciful Father, on this day we remember your gentle virgin martyr, Agnes, at once fearless and faithful to you, in the face of cruelty and awful provocation. For one so young, her example speaks to those more mature in age as a model of steadfastness and sacrificial dedication to you, for which we give you our thanks.
Amen

224 **24 January**
Francis de Sales, Bishop of Geneva, teacher of the faith (1622)

Lord God, we remember this day your servant Francis, who preached with great love and understanding, patience and gentleness. May his devotion to you and his guidance on the devotional life be helpful to us in our own prayers and meditation.
Amen

225 **28 January**
Thomas Aquinas, priest, philosopher and teacher of the faith (1274)

Lord of all, we celebrate today a man of learning and prayer, Thomas Aquinas, universal teacher and 'Angelic doctor' of letters. We give thanks for his gifts of teaching and theological wisdom and for his ability to communicate your Word through homilies and hymns.
Amen

226 **30 January**
Charles, king and martyr (1649)

Almighty God, we remember today a temporal king, whose pride helped to bring about his martyrdom, but whose faith was undoubted. Help us to avoid the strife

between Christians which led to his death and to discern your will and judgement in accepting difference, but withstanding relativism.
Amen

227 **3 February**
Anskar, Archbishop of Hamburg, missionary in Denmark and Sweden (865)

Empowering God, you gave your servant Anskar great responsibility over your Church in Denmark, Norway and Sweden. We celebrate today his energy and sacrificial way of life, together with his dedication to the poor, to education and to the transforming power of preaching.
Amen

228 **14 February**
Cyril and Methodius, apostles to the Slavs, Patrons of Europe (869 and 885)

Lord of faithfulness and companionship, today we remember and celebrate the brothers Cyril and Methodius, apostles to the Slavs, patriotic and scholarly. We rejoice in the Cyrillic language and translation work which they achieved and the ecumenism they fostered.
Amen

229 **17 February**
Janani Luwum, Archbishop of Uganda, martyr (1977)

God of mercy, today we remember your servant and martyr, Janani Luwum, whose witness in the face of tyranny in Uganda led to his martyrdom. We thank you, Lord, for his enthusiasm for the good news of Jesus and for his outspokenness against evil.
Amen

230 **27 February**
George Herbert, priest and poet (1633)

Sublime Lord, may we praise you, as George Herbert did, seven whole days, not one in seven. Today we give thanks for his life and work, as a conscientious country parson and a poet with the words of an angel, as contemporary today as when he put pen to paper.
Amen

231 **1 March**
David (Dewi), Bishop of Menevia, Patron of Wales (c 601)

Almighty God, we give thanks today for the inspiration of your servant David, founder of monasteries and Patron Saint of Wales. May his example of kindness and compassion, simple living and persuasive preaching bring us to a right relationship with you, living, loving Lord.
Amen

232 **7 March**
Perpetua, Felicity, and their companions, martyrs, at Carthage (203)

Lord of hope, we thank you for the inspiration of your servants Perpetua, Felicity and their companions, who died at Carthage for their faith and remained strong in that faith even to death. We remember the distress of leaving young ones behind and of seeing companions torn to pieces by leopards, but wonder at the courage and beliefs shown in the face of unimaginable cruelty.
Amen

233 **8 March**
Edward King, Bishop of Lincoln (1910)

Lord God, caring Saviour, we celebrate today the life and ministry of Edward King, revered for his holiness and pastoral awareness. We especially remember his abilities as teacher and theologian, together with his example as caring bishop to clergy and laity alike.
Amen

234 **17 March**
Patrick, bishop, missionary, Patron of Ireland (c 460)

Almighty and overarching God, today we praise your name for your gift of Patrick who, though abducted from his homeland into slavery in Ireland and managing to escape, nevertheless returned there as missionary and bishop. Through his supplications and deep pastoral care you gave him the skills to evangelise and become Patron of Ireland, securing the faith for future generations, for which we give you thanks.
Amen

235 **20 March**
Cuthbert, Bishop of Lindisfarne, missionary (687)
– commemorated in some traditions on 4 September

We thank you on this day for the life of Cuthbert, inspired at the death of Aidan to heed your call. We remember his gifts of healing and prophecy which, together with his zeal for teaching, visiting and preaching, gave to Lindisfarne a special place in English Christianity, and Cuthbert a special place in your kingdom as his life came to an end on his beloved Farne Island.
Amen

236 **21 March**
Thomas Cranmer, Archbishop of Canterbury, Reformation martyr (1556) – in Wales, commemorated jointly with Hugh Latimer, Nicholas Ridley and Robert Ferrar

Today we offer our thanks for the great contribution of Thomas Cranmer, Archbishop of Canterbury and martyr, to the knowledge, understanding and practice of our faith. For the Book of Common Prayer, for the Ordinal and for the Thirty-nine Articles we owe him a debt of gratitude – and remember today his martyrdom and his bold final statement of faith at the stake.
Amen

237 10 April

William Law, priest, spiritual writer (1761)

Lord of devotion and integrity, on this day we honour the life, writings and ministry of William Law, a man of learning and prayer, who led others into the path of faith and meditation. May we follow his path of truth and obedience, which takes us to you.
Amen

238 23 April

George, martyr, Patron of England (c 304)

God of triumph and sacrifice, we give thanks today for the life and legacy of George, martyr and patron of the Byzantine armies, whose fame as a soldier and peaceful helper against evil forces became so potent in England and beyond. May we take heart from his bravery and rejoice at his deeds, legendary and factual, over dragons and evil.
Amen

239 25 April

Mark, evangelist (first century)

God of the gospel, we give thanks for the life of Mark, evangelist and companion to Paul and Barnabas, the first to record the gospel account. May we learn from his directness, his energy, and his faithfulness to the events he witnessed and wrote about.
Amen

240 1 May

Philip and James 'the less', apostles (first century)
– commemorated in some traditions on 3 May

Today let us recall with thanksgiving the lives, mission and ministry of Philip and James, apostles beloved of Jesus and known for their servant hearts. May we remember their deeds and words as we celebrate their memory and legacy.
Amen

241 **2 May**
Athanasius, Bishop of Alexandria, teacher of the faith (373)

Lord God, Father, Son, and Holy Spirit, on this day we recognise the major contribution of your servant Athanasius, tireless advocate for the faith, in the face of theological turmoil. We remember especially his championing of the Trinity, his scholarship and his commitment to the people of Alexandria.
Amen

242 **8 May**
Julian of Norwich, spiritual writer (c 1417)

Loving Lord, on this day we offer our thanks and praise for the revelations of your love shown to Julian of Norwich. May we gain an insight through the writings she has left for our lasting benefit.
Amen

243 **14 May**
Matthias, apostle and evangelist (first century)

Heavenly Father, on this day may we remember the life and devotion of Matthias, recognised by his fellow disciples when he was chosen by lot to replace Judas Iscariot as the twelfth apostle. May we always be as faithful, ready to fulfil any role you may ask of us.
Amen

244 **19 May**
Dunstan, Archbishop of Canterbury (988)

Lord of change and continuity, on this day we remember the life and work of your servant Dunstan, called to restore and develop your Church and monasteries in England. May his example as a great Archbishop of Canterbury encourage present Archbishops in their task of restoration and renewal.
Amen

245 **20 May**
Alcuin, deacon, Abbot of Tours (804)

Loving Lord, we thank you for the life and work of Alcuin, deacon, who devoted his life to religious and educational matters, as writer, adviser, and master and Abbot of Tours. May we value and mark his contributions, which advanced our understanding of your kingdom.
Amen

246 **24 May**
John and Charles Wesley, evangelists, hymn writers (1791 and 1788)

Wonderful Counsellor, Almighty God, we give thanks on this day for the creative, tireless mission and ministry of John and Charles Wesley, whose hearts were moved by your Holy Spirit to a life of evangelism through prayer, preaching and praise. May we feel our hearts warmed by your presence and our lives be inspired by their service to you and your Church.
Amen

247 **26 May**
Augustine, first Archbishop of Canterbury (605) – commemorated in some traditions on 27 May

God of purpose and vision, on this day we celebrate the life and mission of Augustine, first Archbishop of Canterbury, sent by Pope Gregory to re-evangelise the English Church. May we rejoice at his successful establishment of the Church in Canterbury, Rochester, and then in London, and give thanks.
Amen

248 **30 May**
Josephine Butler, social reformer (1906)

We give thanks for the reforming zeal of Josephine Butler, who fought injustice for marginalised women, as your Son did. May the power of her prayer and social action inspire us and future generations to justice, love, mercy and walking with you, our God.
Amen

249 **5 June**
Boniface (Wynfrith) of Crediton, bishop, apostle of Germany, martyr (754)

Almighty God, you conferred great courage and learning on your servant Boniface, whom we remember and celebrate today. As we recall his ministry as missionary, bishop and reformer, may we gain insight and encouragement in our understanding of your purpose for us today.
Amen

250 **9 June**
Columba, Abbot of Iona, missionary (597)

On this day we give thanks for the ministry and mission of Columba, austere yet loving, energetic yet prayerful, who brought Christianity from Ireland to Scotland and the north of England. May we wonder at his impact and be inspired by his legacy.
Amen

251 **11 June**
Barnabas, apostle (first century)

Lord of all, on this day let us recall the pioneering missionary work of Barnabas, especially in Cyprus as founder of the Church there. May we take heart and inspiration from the zeal of his ministry and the energy of his mission.
Amen

252 **16 June**
Richard of Chichester, bishop (1253)
– commemorated in some traditions on 3 April

As we remember the life, ministry and writings of your servant, Richard of Chichester, may we seek always to know you more clearly, love you more dearly and follow you more nearly, day by day. Let his work inspire us in our daily lives.
Amen

253 **23 June**
Etheldreda, queen, foundress and Abbess of Ely (c 679)

Lord of dedication and holiness, we honour the life and memory of your servant Etheldreda, who served both Crown and Church with distinction and patience. May we show her dedication and desire to spread your word in our own intercessions and spiritual life.
Amen

254 **24 June**
The birth of John the Baptist

God of beginnings and endings, we celebrate today the birth of John, the forerunner of Christ, who gave encouragement to the people of God and prepared them for the arrival of the Messiah, our Redeemer. May we gain confidence from John's life and works as we mark the beginning of his pivotal role in the Christian story.
Amen

255 **28 June**
Irenaeus, Bishop of Lyons, teacher of the faith (c 200)

God of tough love, today we celebrate the life and work of Irenaeus, bishop, theologian and reconciler, whose rigours of scholarship safeguarded the foundation of the faith. Let us be thankful for the benefits of his understanding and learning in our own journey of faith.
Amen

256 **29 June**
Peter and Paul, apostles (c 65)

Lord of great gifting, we give thanks on this special day for the two towers of strength to your Son's ministry and mission, Peter the 'rock' and Paul, the 'apostle to the Gentiles'. May we acknowledge our debt of gratitude to their humanity and their dedication and commitment to spread the good news, even to death.
Amen

257 **3 July**
Thomas, apostle (first century)
– commemorated in some traditions on 21 December

Our Lord and our God, we honour today the life and work of mission of Thomas, apostle, who wanted confirmation of the resurrection, but in receiving the evidence from Jesus became a fearless advocate for the Way, the Truth and the Life. May we who have not seen but believe thank you for the openness and honesty of Thomas, whose doubt enabled Jesus to banish all doubt.
Amen

258 **11 July**
Benedict, abbot, patriarch of the Western monks (c 547)

Lord of community, on this day we remember Benedict, author of the 'Rule for Monks', which has guided the conduct of monasteries over the centuries. May his prudence, moderation and obedience be a model for our relationship with each other today, as we seek your kingdom, by your grace.
Amen

259 **14 July**
John Keble, priest, tractarian poet (1866)

We remember today the gifts and talents of John Keble, poet and tractarian, a prime mover of the Oxford movement, who remained faithful to the high church principles of the Church of England. We give thanks for his poetry, his spiritual guidance and his ministry, which have inspired the Church even to this day.
Amen

260 **15 July**
Swithun, Bishop of Winchester (c 862)

We recall on this day the ministry and charitable works of Swithun, Bishop of Winchester, builder of churches and exemplar of Christian simplicity and holiness. Help us to remember his life in your service when we look out for rain on this date.
Amen

261 **19 July**
Gregory of Nyssa, bishop, and his sister Macrina, deaconess, teachers of the faith (394 and 379)

God of authority and insights, today we celebrate the life and wisdom of Gregory of Nyssa, one of the Cappadocian fathers responsible for building up the foundation beliefs of the Church, and his sister Macrina, whose spiritual depth influenced him. May we wonder at their powers of theological understanding and ability to transmit this to others.
Amen

262 **22 July**
Mary Magdalene (first century)

God of forgiveness and revelation, we remember with grateful thanks the faithfulness of Mary Magdalene, repentant sinner, who stood by your Son at his death and was there to witness to his resurrection and give the good news to his disciples. May we have the faith, the loyalty and the perseverance of Mary in our faith journey – and rejoice in hers.
Amen

263 **25 July**
James, apostle and martyr (44)

We celebrate the apostle James, present with Jesus at the transfiguration and at Gethsemane and martyred on the orders of Herod Agrippa. May his zeal and impetuosity be both a spur and a lesson to us in our demonstration of faith.
Amen

264 **26 July**
Anne and Joachim, parents of the Blessed Virgin Mary

God of great faithfulness, we thank you on this day for Anne and Joachim, parents of the mother of your Son. May their lives be an example of the importance of a holy education for our children.
Amen

265 **29 July**
Mary, Martha and Lazarus, companions of our Lord (first century) – in some traditions only Martha is commemorated

God of great generosity, on this day we commemorate Martha, Mary and Lazarus, who among them looked after Jesus in different ways, showing both affection and loyalty when others deserted him. May we show in our lives the same sense of service to you, Lord.
Amen

266 **30 July**
William Wilberforce, social reformer (1833)

God of great objectives, we commemorate the oratorical skills and the campaigning, evangelical determination of William Wilberforce, who led the movement to abolish slavery. May we be inspired by his single-mindedness and his perseverance in pursuing this endeavour successfully.
Amen

267 **5 August**
Oswald, King of Northumbria, martyr (642)
– commemorated in some traditions on 8 or 9 August

God of great endeavour, we recall on this day the feats of fortitude of Oswald, King of Northumbria, in defence of Christendom, working in partnership with Aidan. Let us give thanks for his skill and bravery in battle and his wisdom in faith and leadership.
Amen

268 **8 August**
Dominic, founder of the Order of the Franciscan Preachers (1221)

God of truth and light, we give thanks that you sent your servant Dominic to spread your word and practise your Son's teaching to such great effect. May his impact and the order he founded continue to influence our daily lives and learning in modern times.
Amen

269 **9 August**
Mary Elizabeth Sumner, founder of the Mothers' Union (1921)

God our Father, you gave to Mary the sacred job of becoming the mother of your Son. On this day we remember with gratitude the vision and perseverance of

Mary Sumner in explaining and encouraging the principles of Christian family life, both nationally and internationally. May we seek to support and sustain that vision as the bedrock of our society today and tomorrow.
Amen

270 **11 August**
Clare of Assisi, founder of the Minoresses or Poor Clares (1253)

On this day we recall and honour the contemplative life and devotion of Clare of Assisi, inspired by Francis and having an influence spreading across Europe through the founding of convents. Let her example show how the light of Christ can shine brightly through faith and such holiness.
Amen

271 **13 August**
Jeremy Taylor, Bishop of Down and Connorteacher of the faith (1667)

Lord of inclusion and diversity, on this day we acknowledge the lucidity of thought and active engagement of Jeremy Taylor in his life and writing. May we learn from the way he took things on – and took opponents on – but also be aware of the costs.
Amen

272 **15 August**
The Blessed Virgin Mary
– commemorated in some traditions on 8 September

Father God, today we honour and venerate the life of Mary, the mother of your Son, whose humility and obedience brought about the revelation of your relationship with humankind through your Son. May we wonder at her faithfulness and rejoice at her response to your calling.
Amen

273 **20 August**
Bernard, Abbot of Clairvaux, teacher of the faith (1153)

God of order and worth, we remember and celebrate the work and influence of Bernard of Clairvaux, who gave the Cistercian Order a new impetus across Europe. We thank you that, through his insights and efforts, he has influenced so many lives today.
Amen

274 **24 August**
Bartholomew, apostle (first century)

God of great reach, we honour the apostle Bartholomew, who witnessed the miracle of the resurrection and who spread the gospel far and wide. Let us, like Bartholomew, see and believe through the witness of the disciples.
Amen

275 **27 August**
Monica, mother of Augustine of Hippo (387)

Lord of love and influence, let us rejoice at the patient care and persistent prayers of Monica, who never gave up on her wayward son, Augustine, and whose love was rewarded by his conversion and subsequent ministry. Bless all parents who seek the right balance between letting go and showing tough love.
Amen

276 **28 August**
Augustine of Hippo, bishop, teacher of the faith (430)

Great God, we offer you our thanks and praise for the life, works and ministry of Augustine of Hippo, who revealed your grace through his humanity and his writings. May we be informed and inspired by his special insights into your reconciling love for the world in and through Christ.
Amen

277 **29 August**
The beheading of John the Baptist
– see under June 24 for the birth of John the Baptist

God of true promise, on this day we remember the sacrifice of John the Baptist, who always heralded and acknowledged Jesus as Lord, even unto death. Never let us underestimate the importance of his ministry and his message of the freedom of heavenly peace.
Amen

278 **30 August**
John Bunyan, spiritual writer (1688)

Master, friend, Saviour, may we rejoice at the inspiring life and work of John Bunyan, writer of Pilgrim's Progress, who saw that the world was full of spiritual warfare. May we never flinch from his message and from your grace abounding in bringing us salvation.
Amen

279 **3 September**
Gregory the Great, pope, teacher of the faith (604)

God of great enterprise, today we mark the life, ministry and inspiration of Gregory the Great, pope, pastor and principal architect of the re-evangelisation of England. As we rejoice in the Church today and face the challenges ahead, may we take heart from his achievements and his devotion to your will.
Amen

280 **8 September**
The birth of the Blessed Virgin Mary, the mother of Jesus Christ

Father God, on this day we rejoice at the birth of the Blessed Virgin Mary, the mother of your Son, Jesus Christ, and wonder at her faith and fortitude. Endow us with the patience and the care she showed in all that she did and all that she was and remains for us now.
Amen

281 **13 September**
John Chrysostom, Bishop of Constantinople, teacher of the faith (407)

We give thanks today for the reforming zeal of John Chrysostom and his ability to communicate important Christian messages in relevant ways. Let his forthright insights and practical approach be appreciated as much in present times as they were in his day.
Amen

282 **14 September**
Holy Cross Day

On this day we commemorate the discovery of the cross of Christ by Helena, the mother of Emperor Constantine, and rejoice at this universal symbol of the Christian Church. Let it always inspire and inform our lives and our journey of faith.
Amen

283 **15 September**
Cyprian, Bishop of Carthage, martyr (258)
– commemorated in some traditions on 16 or 26 September

God of great compassion, we thank you today for the pastoral compassion and courage of Cyprian, who sought the unity of the Church and resisted pagan practices imposed by the emperor. Help us to retain pastoral sensitivities in the face of secular provocation.
Amen

284 **16 September**
Ninian, bishop and missionary (fifth century)

God of far and wide, we recall with gratitude the influence of Ninian on the Picts and on Whithorn, where he built a church. In honouring his memory may we commit ourselves to leaving a mark in your world to advance your kingdom and to your praise and glory.
Amen

285 **17 September**
Hildegard, Abbess of Bingen, visionary (1179)

God of visions and radiance, today we commemorate the inspiring life and work of Hildegard of Bingen, abbess and visionary, who brought us pure glimpses of your creation. May we always allow you to return to the centre of our lives, however far we stray, recognising that we owe our very existence to you alone.
Amen

286 **20 September**
John Coleridge Patteson, first Bishop of Melanesia, and his companions, martyrs (1871)

God of hope and sacrifice, today we recall with thanks the great work of mission in the Pacific islands of John Coleridge Patteson and his companions, cruelly killed in revenge for the actions of European slave traders. May their work live on in the work of the Church in Melanesia today.
Amen

287 **21 September**
Matthew, apostle and evangelist (first century)

God of the Gospels, today we recall and honour Matthew, evangelist and apostle, who swapped worldly wealth for poverty at the call of Jesus, but who then captured the greatest story ever told in his gospel account. May we wonder at the miraculous way this man who was regarded as a publican and sinner was transformed through your Son's call.
Amen

288 **25 September**
Lancelot Andrewes, Bishop of Winchester, spiritual writer (1626)

Today we celebrate the life and works of your servant Lancelot, who through his preaching, writings, translating and pastoral ministry, brought many people closer to your kingdom. Let your light continue to shine through his example.
Amen

289 **27 September**
Vincent de Paul, founder (1660)

Lord of love and mercy, today we honour the selfless ministry of Vincent de Paul, whose life was transformed through his experience of helping the outcasts of society and who sought to bring this austerity into the heart of the Church's work. Let that mission continue in his tradition in present times and needs.
Amen

290 **29 September**
Michael and All Angels

God of angelic powers, we commemorate today the role of your angels Michael, Gabriel and Raphael as instruments of your will and guardians of Christians over the centuries. May we expect your angels anywhere we go, knowing they are keeping watch for you.
Amen

291 **4 October**
Francis of Assisi, friar, deacon, founder of the Friars Minor (1226)

We celebrate the life and works of Francis of Assisi with the awe and wonder he felt for your creation, Lord. Let his founding of the Friars Minor, the Poor Ladies and the Tertiaries be a legacy of his devotion to you and his commitment to building Christian communities.
Amen

292 **6 October**
William Tyndale, translator of the Scriptures, Reformation martyr (1536)

God of the Scriptures, on this day we honour and celebrate the groundbreaking and sacrificial achievements of William Tyndale, who made the Bible accessible to all by his masterly translation. Let his legacy be that we can understand your Word and learn your ways with a directness that brings us closer to you.
Amen

293 **10 October**
Paulinus of York, bishop. missionary (644)

Lord of great missions, today we celebrate the calling and achievements of Paulinus of York, who established the Church in many areas in the north of England and brought skills of diplomacy and authority to the task. We rejoice at his legacy and example of vocation and mission.
Amen

294 **13 October**
Edward the Confessor, King of England (1066)

God of grandeur, on this day we recall with gratitude the generosity and holiness of a peace-loving monarch, Edward the Confessor, who reigned in difficult times, but left a legacy in endowing Westminster Abbey. When we enter that place, may we draw inspiration from his vision and his devotion to you, Lord.
Amen

295 **15 October**
Teresa of Avila, religious, foundress, mystic, teacher of the faith (1582)

Lord of vision and love, today we rejoice at the insights and mystical experiences of your servant Teresa of Avila and wonder at her ability to combine them with the harsh

round of work, prayer and penance, integrating them in her writings. We praise you for the illumination they shine on our own lives of prayer and service.
Amen

296 **17 October**
Ignatius, Bishop of Antioch, martyr (c 107)

God of triumph and sacrifice, on this day we recall the writings and martyrdom of Ignatius, Bishop of Antioch, in the early Church, resolute in faith and encouraging to other Christians to the last. Let his commitment to you in the face of persecution be an encouragement to us in the face of indifference.
Amen

297 **18 October**
Luke, evangelist (first century)

God of the Gospels, we give thanks on this day for the faithful witnessing and recording of Luke in his Gospel and in the Acts of the Apostles. May we be grateful for the clarity and artistry of his writing and the generous insights into your Son's ministry that he has left for us.
Amen

298 **28 October**
Simon and Jude, apostles (first century)

Lord of friendship and fellowship, on this day we remember the apostles Simon and Jude, faithful disciples who preached the good news in Persia and died there witnessing to the faith. Help us to understand that you are never a lost cause, even when the world says you are.
Amen

299 29 October
James Hannington, Bishop of Eastern Equatorial Africa, martyr in Uganda (1885)

We recall the pioneering missions of James Hannington, first Bishop of Eastern Equatorial Africa, who sought to extend your kingdom into Uganda and died in the process. May we always take risks for you, as your Son did for us.
Amen

300 1 November
All Saints (All Hallows)

Today we give thanks for all the heroes of the faith who have inspired others to faith and holiness. May we rejoice in the cloud of witnesses to the faith your Son taught us, seeking their intercession and your continued gift of the Holy Spirit to your Church on earth.
Amen

301 3 November
Richard Hooker, Anglican apologist, teacher (1600)
– commemorated in some traditions on 30 October

God of Scripture and tradition, on this day we recall the scholarship and reconciling ministry of Richard Hooker, who showed that different strands of Anglicanism could be held together in harmony. May his wisdom and far-sightedness be seen as part of our church life today, to honour his life and witness.
Amen

302 7 November
Willibrord of York, Archbishop of Utrecht, apostle of Frisia (739)

God of great ambition, today we mark the energetic ministry of Willibrord, an English priest who became Patron Saint of the Netherlands by his missionary zeal and

his skilful church organisation. May we celebrate his great achievements in Europe, paving the way for Boniface and others to follow.
Amen

303 8 November
The saints and martyrs of England/The saints of Wales

Lord of love and sacrifice, may we mark today the contributions of men and women from these islands who are beacons of hope in bringing the good news to people of different lands, including our own. As we remember them collectively let us honour them individually, in your name.
Amen

304 10 November
Leo the Great, pope (461)

Almighty God, on this day we give thanks for the life and work of Leo the Great, doctor and preserver of the faith, who faithfully protected Rome and the true faith from various assaults of the enemies. May we be equally resolute in defending the faith today, Lord.
Amen

305 11 November
Martin of Tours (c 397)

God of great works, we celebrate today the fearless ministry of Martin of Tours, both his missionary zeal and his example of Christian discipleship. Give us too the courage and ambition to attempt great things for you.
Amen

306 13 November
Charles Simeon, priest, evangelical divine (1836)

Loving Lord, we recall today the powerful preaching and evangelical commitment of Charles Simeon, who helped shape the Church and helped found the CMS. May his zeal to show the redeeming love of God be a lasting legacy to us all.
Amen

307 17 November
Hugh, Bishop of Lincoln (1200)

Lord of all virtues, we thank you that Hugh, Bishop of Lincoln, came to England to revive first a monastery, then a cathedral and a diocese. May his zeal be recognised and his legacy be respected.
Amen

308 18 November
Elizabeth of Hungary, princess, widow and philanthropist (1231)

God of humility and service, today we thank you for the life and ministry of your servant Elizabeth of Hungary, whose fortunes rose and fell, but whose faith was constant. Let us take heart from her continued desire to serve you though love and obedience, however harsh her circumstances.
Amen

309 19 November
Hilda, Abbess of Whitby (680)
– commemorated in some traditions on 17 November

Mighty Counsellor, we offer thanks and praise today for the wonderful ministry of Hilda, Abbess of Whitby, called to be a religious and to oversee the double monastery of Whitby, where she hosted the important Synod of Whitby. May we acknowledge and admire the great influence of Hilda on the Anglo-Saxon Church.
Amen

310 20 November
Edmund, King of the East Angles, martyr (870)

Almighty God, we thank you for giving courage and resolve to Edmund, King of the East Angles, whom we commemorate today. As a martyr who died refusing to deny his faith, let us not forget his story and his contribution to the English Church.
Amen

311 30 November
Andrew the Apostle (first century)

God of great missions, we give thanks today for the missionary initiatives and zeal of the apostle Andrew, called from his nets to follow your Son and bringing with him Simon Peter, the rock on which your Church was built. May Andrew's encouragement and persistence in mission be a constant reminder of our responsibility as your followers to help others 'come and see'.
Amen

312 6 December
Nicholas, Bishop of Myra (fourth century)

Lord of generosity and celebration, we rejoice today at the life and legend of Nicholas, who gave generously and cared for many, especially children. As we look forward to Christmas, let us acknowledge his influence on our present-day celebrations.
Amen

313 8 December
The conception of the Blessed Virgin Mary

God of wonder, help us today to take in the full enormity of the journey begun in the conception of Mary and taking us through to the incarnation of your Son, the Messiah. May our sense of awe combine with your many signs and

signals through the prophets to give us confidence, hope and excitement at the prospect of that journey's destination.
Amen

314 **13 December**
Lucy, martyr of Syracuse (304)

God of faith and sacrifice, we remember today the devotion of Lucy to the true faith, despite the pain and suffering she endured. Let the light of her courage shine like a beacon on those who remain faithful in the face of such forces.
Amen

315 **26 December**
Stephen, deacon and first martyr (c 35)

On this day we give thanks for the life and martyrdom of Stephen, whose wisdom and spirit in preaching the gospel led to his stoning. We pray that his example of selfless courage shines as a beacon to us all.
Amen

316 **27 December**
John, apostle and evangelist (c100)

We pray for the memory of John, evangelist and apostle, who was present at the Transfiguration, experienced the Last Supper, witnessed the Crucifixion, stood by Mary in her grief, and saw and believed the Resurrection. We give thanks for John's loyalty and devotion, his deep and rich faith, and the ability to communicate it, to your glory. We ask this through your Son, Jesus Christ.
Amen

317 28 December
The Holy Innocents

We give thanks today for those innocent young ones who died at Herod's whim. Mistaken for a threat to the world, they died for the Saviour of the world. May they be thanked and thanked again, in heaven and on earth, and never forgotten, through the grace of the one whom Herod did not reach, the one who would have reached out to him, your Son, Jesus Christ.
Amen

318 29 December
Thomas Becket, Archbishop of Canterbury and martyr (1170) – commemorated in some traditions on 7 July

God of peace, we commend and celebrate the life of Thomas Becket, cut short in Canterbury Cathedral, for which act Henry made due penitence. We draw courage and comfort from Thomas' openness and vulnerability; from the pilgrimages made over the ages to mark his martyrdom: and from the inspiration of your Son in all that Thomas did in your name.
Amen

THE HOLY SPIRIT AND THE SPIRITUAL

319 We thank you, Lord, for calling us to be your servants and disciples.
Strengthen us, we pray, in our powers to listen and learn and to be open to the Holy Spirit.
Deepen our trust in your love for us at all times and in all places.
May we never try to hide from you or deny your name.
And let the light of your Son's life and teachings illuminate our path
and shine forth in our lives.
Amen

320 In a world where hope has sometimes been scattered to the four winds,
bring your Holy Spirit alive to those who seek a way forward, not a step back.
Let people of faith in the future hold sway over those who rail against the present
and may the lessons of the past be understood and learnt.
In the world of today we pray for the people and places suffering through natural as well as man-made events, especially . . .
Amen

321 As we admire the night sky we see that the stars shine still,
yet they are moving as they shine,
just as the Holy Spirit moves within us and around us,
going where he will, prompting, encouraging and empowering.
Let that Holy Spirit roam across town and country,
forest and desert, continents and islands,
so that the world is truly aware of its origins
and the need to sustain your creation
through human ingenuity and careful stewardship.
Bring hope and help where needed, whether practically, politically, spiritually.
Amen

322 Let us pray for our Church nationally
and for this church, in which we worship your name.
May our leaders be strengthened by your Holy Spirit;
may our buildings be blessed by your peace;

may your people be empowered to deepen their faith.
And may we learn from Christians in other lands
where there is often persecution;
where there is frequently greater attendance;
and where there is sometimes prayer for us.
So let us join with them in our communion
at the breaking of the bread.
Amen

323 Lord of mind and spirit,
give us a true appreciation of celestial sounds,
in music, in voice, in words, in prayer.
May the gift of silence crowd out the sound of noise.
May we value balance in all things,
rhythm in most things,
and harmony as well as melody.
Amen

324 God of vision and purpose,
give us the goal of meeting our potential,
in a world where you have shown
that nothing is impossible with you.
Put us to work to your greater glory.
And along the way may we appreciate
the joys of excellence
in those who have practised and sharpened their skills,
spiritually and physically, to your glory.
Amen

325 Lord God,
bringer of music and mystery,
of Olympic talents,
of great works of literature,
of amazing feats of endurance,
let us be inspired to understand you
in the achievements of others;
in the example of friends;
in our own talents,
begun, continued and culminated
in your love for us.
Amen

326 God of soul and spirit,
lift our hearts through music and song
and bring me to tears,
in joy as well as sadness.
We ask for your blessings on music and musicians,
on all who feed our soul
and touch our spirit
with sacred music,
the beat of angels' wings,
and the sound of the spheres.
Amen

327 Lord of life and rhythm,
stretch our senses through music and movement,
in the way we respond to music
and through the gifts of your great goodness.
May our spirits soar
as the notes of music and musicians,
sacred and secular,
set our minds free
and our imaginations running.
Amen

328 God of peace and perfection,
may the melody and harmony of music
connect with the pull of our heartstrings
and the fondness of memories,
from 'madeleine' moments
to loves lost and won.
Set us searching for these
through chords and choruses,
through instruments and voices,
always remembering the origins
of their creative spark.
Amen

329 God of glory,
may we appreciate the silence between notes,
the calm between the storms,
and the light in the midst of darkness.
Let music refine our sense of you,
as it defines our understanding of ourselves.
We thank you for the inspiration
of composition
and the mastery of musicians in their craft.
Amen

330 Searching Lord,
may we respond to your open arms
through the spirit of music
as well as the power of the word.
In worship and praise
let us sing out our love for you.
And in the gifts you have bestowed on musicians
may we see your love at work,
in note and form,
in tempo and timing.
Amen

331 God of scripture,
give your creative spirit to all who write;
may they capture the truth they seek to explain.
Illuminate their thoughts with the light of love,
and provide them with the right words
to express their thoughts and feelings.
Amen

332 Creator God,
help us to read into the minds of those who write.
May we glimpse their insights
as we rejoice in their words.
Let the things we read and learn
inform our thinking
and lead us to balanced views
and deeper thoughts,

as well as enjoyable moments.
Let your love shine
through the prism of the printed page
and the magic of the screen.
Amen

333 Liberating Lord,
set our minds free from routine thoughts
as we enter the world of imagination,
either our own as we seek the creative spark,
or through the minds of others,
as we read their work or see their vision.
Save us from going through the motions,
as we engage our inmost yearnings.
Amen

334 Lord of spirit and truth,
surround our thoughts and hopes
with meditation and contemplation.
As we seek to make sense of the world,
through poetry and prayer,
through word and deed,
through music and song,
may your spirit spark
exploration of the gift of imagination,
in writer, reader and viewer alike.
What a wonderful world!
Amen

335 Heavenly Father,
may we write on a wing and a prayer,
as we explore your world
through the imagination of our hearts and minds.
Bring us the ability to interpret and test,
through our reading and writing.
May your Holy Bible be the fount of wisdom
and the backdrop to all our musing.
And may the writers of today
acknowledge their debt – and ours – to your Word.
Amen

CREATION

God's generosity

336 God of true riches,
may we not build up treasure for its own sake or to impress others,
but use it wisely and for the sake of many.
Let us remember that the gifts we have received came from you
and are for the orphan and widow,
the neighbour and stranger, as well as ourselves.
Lift up all who praise your name
and use us all to do your will.
Amen

337 Wonderful Counsellor, mighty judge
and generous guardian of righteousness,
we pray that in our lives, as in our thoughts,
we may show to others
the steadfastness and encouragement
you have shown to us.
May we share in the hope that John prepared us for,
starting with our own repentance and righteousness.
Grant to your people a desire for change,
the chance of peace.
Lift our sights to see the full extent of your kingdom,
knowing our capacity to grow and trusting us to do so.
Amen

338 You have called us to come and see,
just as your Son called the disciples
to follow him and recruit others to the Way.
May we be responsive and committed, always learning,
always alert to the needs of others,
always focused on our relationship with you, Father God.
Amen

339 God of our foundations, may we draw on your wisdom as we seek to build your kingdom.
Give us the will to persevere and the insight
to see the meaning of your creation.

We have the second chance your Son has given us
to make things right in our relationship with you.
Only let us reconnect.
Amen

340 Father of all, God of firm foundations,
give us, we pray, the power to do good and resist evil.
Whatever is thrown at us or we come up against,
strengthen our resolve to do your will
and to walk humbly with our God
who will save us from flood and tempest, wind and rain,
and bring us home.
Amen

341 Harness us to your yoke, we pray,
so that we may share your burden.
When we fail, you are there; when you call, we can assist,
confident that you are leading us in the right direction,
whose service is perfect freedom.
May you reach out, with our help,
to those who are yet to know you,
even though you already know them.
Let openness and inclusion mark our witness
and honour your offer of salvation to all who turn to you.
Amen

342 Gracious Lord,
you are full of compassion, full of kindness and truth.
Grant us, we pray, the strength to resist evil,
the ability to distinguish good seed from bad
and the capacity to listen to you at all times.
May our hope be in you, our trust in your Son,
and our inspiration be your Holy Spirit.
May we be children of God in your eyes,
keen to grow in faith and ready to learn.
Amen

343 Father God,
we know we cannot be separated from the love of Christ.
Nor can we be parted from the pearl of great value
once we have acknowledged you as our Lord and master.
Allow us, we pray, to worship you
as our maker, our mentor, our muse.
Send us out to proclaim your word,
as your Son taught us, as you commanded,
and as your Holy Spirit has empowered us.
Amen

344 O God our provider,
you listen to our complaints with long-suffering patience,
knowing the difference between our wants and our needs.
Grant us the serenity to accept the outcome of these complaints,
which you will respond to in your time, not ours.
Give us inner strength to carry on through difficulties
in the sure and certain hope that you are there
when things get really tough,
as those footsteps in the sand showed, where you carried us.
Amen

345 Trusting God,
you have shown faith in us
by sending your Son to be our Saviour.
Give us the strength of faith to follow you
without being diverted by the pressures and temptations of the world.
Let the abundance of the life your Son has promised
be centred on you, Lord,
starting and ending with divine things
and bringing the human things into perspective.
Amen

346 Give us the boldness, Lord, to love in truth and action.
You have assured us that through obeying your
commandments your Son abides in us and we in him,
with the help of the Holy Spirit.
Amen

347 We give thanks for the promises which have been fulfilled through your Son's ministry.
May we never forget the liberating joy of Easter
and your generosity in persevering with a people
who had let you down.
Let us never feel lost or abandoned in the enfolding love
of a shepherd who always seeks us out and never lets us down.
Amen

348 God of truth and light,
just as Matthias took his place in the twelve, so may we always be seeking the right people to do your will as leaders and role models.
We give thanks for the continuity you have inspired among your people,
following your Son's intervention in the world.
Guide our every action, we pray, Lord,
in the knowledge that you have never let us down, however hard we have tried to ignore you, particularly when things are going well.
Help us to acknowledge your active presence in our lives.
Amen

349 Eternal God,
help us to understand more fully those things we cannot touch and see.
May the Spirit of truth be our guide and the easy pickings of things within our reach be resisted.
Your Son showed us that we can live life both righteously and abundantly.
Give us the confidence, Lord, to stretch ourselves and test ourselves,
knowing that you are there to support and encourage, to forgive and welcome back.
Help us to trust, trust and trust again.
Amen

350 Loving Lord,
help us to be imitators of you, as your children, by forgiving one another and loving you.
In receiving our daily bread may we also seek the bread of life and may we never waiver in our faith,
even when it is tested by temptation to do wrong.
May we follow the path of righteousness, knowing that in Jesus we have the good shepherd who will protect and teach us if we do not stray too far from him.
Amen

351 God of splendour and majesty,
give us wisdom in the way we live our lives,
showing gratitude to you through songs and praises and gaining inspiration through the music of others.
Help us to use our gift of intelligence to understand our faith and communicate the faith.
May we persevere in our learning and our teaching,
in our witness and works, through our heart and mind.
Let hope and gladness fill our souls as we receive the bread of life.
Amen

352 Merciful God,
who spared Nineveh and sent your Son to save us, be our rock as well as our salvation,
our stronghold, fortress and refuge.
Let us never forget how your Son chose the disciples, who suffered much, repented often,
yet steered us through to the faith we have inherited
and which is there for every generation.
You have shown the way to cast our nets, through your Son's example to the disciples.
Give us the will as well as the means to extend your kingdom through our own lives and actions.
May we learn your wisdom, discover your truth and share your word.
May we glimpse your grace as we struggle to understand the full extent of your love for us.
Amen

353 Extravagant God,
we thank you for your generosity
in sending your only Son to be amongst us.
May we be generous in return,
in our praise, in our worship, in our daily lives.
Nothing can compare with the sacrifice made by Jesus
for the sins of all,
but as we track his suffering during Passiontide,
let us renew our commitment to the Christian way,
your way.
Amen

354 God of great expectations,
you have been patient with us
in our understanding of your revelation
through your Son's life, death and resurrection.
Help us to have renewed confidence, firm in faith,
constant in prayer, and attentive in deed.
Strengthen our powers to listen to you
and to proclaim your name, whatever the cost.
May the lives of the saints and martyrs
be an inspiration to our lives and witness.
Amen

355 Heavenly Father,
you have shown the extravagance of your love
by sending your Son to be amongst us.
Help us to appreciate and understand your generosity,
so that in our worship and our praise we seek to do justice
to your grace.
Bestow on us the Spirit of truth
so that we can today truly discern your will for us.
And may we always seek to develop our relationship with you,
even as we learn from others and support each other
in the development of our faith.
Amen

Evolution

356 Creator God,
build up our understanding of your world,
its origins and evolution
its climatic patterns and changes
its geology and geography.
But as we do,
may we step back in wonder
to reflect and give thanks,
to learn from our predecessors,
and to praise your works.
Let the footfall of faith be revealed
and renewed in each generation.
We ask this through the light of the world,
your Son, Jesus Christ.
Amen

357 Lord of all,
create in us a love and respect
for the origins of your world,
so that all we see we honour,
all we touch we explore,
and all we hear we listen to.
Make us curious to know
the length, depth and height of your generosity,
in the life we live,
in the world you made.
May the creative spark that ignited the universe
live in our hearts as well as our minds,
so that our faith grows
as our knowledge is enhanced,
through the one whose love never leaves us,
Jesus Christ.
Amen

358 God of nature and nurture,
bring us a greater understanding of how things evolved,
from the dawn of creation
through to the age of civilization
to the new millennium.
May we acknowledge and embrace progress
but accept that there may be a cost,
in relationships with each other
in our relationship with you.
Restore in us the capacity to wonder.
Renew in us the will to believe.
And let us never cease to strive
to leave the world a better place,
just as your Son did, through whom we pray.
Amen

359 Lord of nature and nurture,
bring us to a true understanding
of the forces at work in the world,
so that we can build a right relationship with you.
Give us hope and confidence
even when the outlook is bleak.
May we do all we can
to minimize climate change
and to allow your creation
to flourish and evolve
as a sign of your greatness
and as a witness to your love,
evergreen God.
Amen

Ecology

360 Heavenly Father,
you have given us balance and challenge
in the environment we take for granted.
May we learn from our mistakes
in our stewardship and duty of care.

Give us the will and the means
to leave the world a better place,
honouring your gift of the ecology we enjoy.
And in everything we see
let us wonder and give thanks,
offering songs of praise,
as well as a witness of silence.
We ask this through your Son, Jesus Christ.
Amen

361 Lord of the environment,
may our surroundings be our spur
to honour all that you have created;
to understand the fragile balance of nature;
to be modest in our use of resources;
and to look for fresh ways to conserve energy.
In our prayers as in our loves,
may your Son be our guide
as we seek to follow his ways,
bringing wholeness and healing
instead of partiality and pain;
and letting go of what is not necessary
in our lives and in our hearts.
Amen

362 Lord,
our surroundings are your home;
make us houseproud for you.
We thank you for sharing it
with us and all creatures great and small.
Give us an insight into the impact of our actions,
for good and ill, on your world,
and on you, forgiving Lord.
Amen

363 Wonderful God,
may we never contain our enthusiasm for your creation,
but may we treat all things
as we would treat a neighbour,
and our neighbours as we would treat ourselves,
for all things are of you.
So let our treatment of our environment
be as if we were treating our relationship with you,
with integrity, honesty and respect,
knowing that you are immanent and omniscient,
yet sensitive to the needs of the least of your creatures.
Amen

Interdependence

364 Creator God,
you have brought together humankind and nature,
interdependent and vulnerable to each other.
Give to us all, we pray,
a sense of proportion and wonder,
a respect for difference and uniqueness.
Let there be amazement at the power of nature,
as your plan is revealed,
as we see your power,
and as we rediscover our care
for all that is in your world.
Amen

365 Lord of all,
help us to love you more,
as we grow in confidence.
Make us more aware of our surroundings,
as we gain knowledge of our place in the world.
Give us space,
but not too much.
Give us resources,
but only what we need.
Give us time,

but only enough to do your will.
Let flora and fauna abound,
so that we can stay around.
Amen

366 Heavenly Father,
leave us with grateful hearts
while we enjoy the flora and fauna of your earth,
especially when we find new uses
for scarce resources,
particularly as we create conservation
for endangered species,
always as we take time to give thanks
for our food and our drink.
Amen

367 God of great gifts,
help us to know when to start,
and when to stop,
in our pursuit of knowledge and understanding
of this world in all its variety.
May we see the wisdom of slowing down,
when our eagerness to achieve
overcomes our need to wonder.
And if we ever fail to do this,
stop us in our tracks, Lord.
Let our imprint be small,
leaving yours as large as nature intended.
Amen

368 God of north and south – as well as east and west,
safeguard the difference and diversity of the poles,
the wildlife, the habitat,
the sea and the ice.
You have wisely separated penguin from polar bear,
but never let us separate your creatures from their
environment.
And may we –
tread softly to protect our dreams;

whisper quietly to honour the silence;
and leave as we found,
gratefully, graciously, gradually.
Amen

Nature and nurture

369 Lord of growth and understanding,
teach us to know,
but also to understand.
Help us to learn by doing,
but grow by observing.
Empower us to build on the gifts you have given us,
so that we can grow in our ability
to pass on what we have learnt
and to model what you want us to be,
as your Son did.
Amen

370 Creator God,
let us know your ways
by observing your Son.
Let us know what to do
by trusting our priests.
Let us grow in understanding
by learning from our mistakes.
Above all, gracious Lord,
equip us to be,
empower us to do,
and enable us to teach,
whatever you need,
so that, at the last,
our nurture and your nature
have guided our journey
and brought us safely home.
Amen

371 Lord of all,
fill us with the knowledge of our nature.
Create in us the capacity for nurture.
Lead us, heavenly Father, lead us,
so that our choices are soundly based,
our decisions forward-focused,
and our guiding light is always your Son,
who restored our nature,
by challenging our nurture,
who welcomed us back
and moved us on,
through your love.
Amen

372 Gracious Lord,
give us the humility to learn,
the ability to grasp new knowledge,
and the desire to pass it on.
We know, Lord, that we are all born with great gifts,
but we forget too easily, Lord,
that we need to sharpen and practise our skills
so that all we do
is done in quiet confidence
that your will is done,
that your kingdom will come.
Amen

373 Heavenly Father,
look on all we do with favour,
where we honour your gifts
and seek to grow our skills.
Send us the ability to cope,
the confidence to hope,
and the need to grow in you
and you in us.
Amen

Climate

374 God of contrast and continuity,
bring us rains to refresh and renew;
bring us sun to warm and nurture;
bring us the wind of your Holy Spirit too.
We give thanks for the delicate balance
of the earth's climate and our daily weather.
May we not upset that balance
by trying to do your work, Lord,
but where natural forces impact on your world,
let us respond to human need,
using the gifts you provide, generous God.
Amen

375 Heavenly Father,
you send the breath of life
through wind and rain and sun.
You send the bread of life
through your only Son.
We give thanks for the climate we depend on,
even when you give us rain
when we want sun.
And even when the snow stops us in our tracks
the weather shows us we can take nothing for granted,
yet everything to be thankful for,
loving Lord.
Amen

376 Almighty God,
ruler of heaven and earth,
who gives us cloud and shade,
who sends us sun and rain,
may we come to appreciate
the sheer variety of climate in the world,
from frozen wastes teeming with life
to tropical forests helping the earth to breathe.
It is not for us to engineer things, Lord,
but let us also not upset climatic balance,

through thoughtless actions and bad stewardship.
Let us be respectful of your creation,
bountiful God.
Amen

377 Lord,
as we travel the world and see your creation,
we also feel the differences in climate
between tropical, temperate and arctic regions.
We may complain about this at times,
but really we rejoice in the difference and diversity.
Thank you for the opportunities we have
to experience the extremes,
but without the privations of previous generations.
May those who live in extremes of climate day by day
continue to be sustained by the resilience you have given them.
And may we all be sensitive to the needs of those who
cannot cope,
Lord of life.
Amen

Natural wonders

378 Almighty God,
we stand in awe of your works all around us,
the smallest and the greatest.
When we see the mountains in sunlight
we give thanks.
When we watch streams and rivers
we see the living water.
When we hear the birdsong at dawn
we feel so privileged.
Give us an appreciation of your generosity
as we go about our daily round
as well as in our travels afar.
Life is a natural wonder
and you have given us the bread of life,
marvellous God, beneficent Father.
Amen

379 Surprising Lord,
who never lets us rest in our journey of life,
open our eyes to the greatness around us.
Help us not to take for granted
that clouds bring rain,
that water brings life,
that the sun brings hope.
Help us safeguard the best of nature,
not just for ourselves,
but for future generations.
Give us the patience that you have shown
in giving us a second chance,
through your Son, our Saviour,
Jesus Christ.
Amen

380 God of power and might,
be gentle with us as we try to scale your mountains,
ride your rivers, fly above your world.
All that you have given us in natural wonders
has pushed the ingenuity and endurance you have also provided
to the limits of our imagination and capacity.
Test us, challenge us, shake us,
so that we can truly appreciate
all you have created
and can take time to thank our creator,
timeless God, eternal Father.
Amen

381 God of imagination,
let the natural wonders speak for themselves
of your glory and generosity.
If we reflect on how they were made,
rivers and seas,
mountains and valleys,
stars and galaxies,
we can only give thanks
that we are alive to see them,

able to study them
and have someone to thank for them,
through your Son, our Saviour, Jesus Christ,
Amen

Natural disasters

382 God of mercy,
you have shown through your Son's pain and sacrifice for us
that you share our suffering.
Look with pity and tears
on the struggles of the people of . . .
as they try to come to terms with what has befallen them.
May all the energies and expertise of humankind
be extended to those affected.
And may those who hurt and those who mourn
be comforted through your presence with them now.
Amen

383 Almighty God,
let the forces unleashed by the earthquake/flood/eruption
in . . .
speak of your power and might.
But may the aftermath testify
to the love you have shown
in sending us your Son.
Let the purpose and resourcefulness
of the survivors and rescuers alike
be united in love for neighbour
and focused on bringing relief and comfort.
May all that you have taught us through your Son
be our motivation and our strength
in responding to need, wherever it shows itself.
And as we do so, Lord,
be alongside the victims in their suffering
and bring hope to their communities.
Amen

384 Lord of compassion,
we stand perplexed as we see
the devastation and suffering
in the aftermath of the . . . in . . .
We know you are in the midst of the pain,
but help us to understand that you did not unleash
the forces that led to this disaster.
We struggle to comprehend but are ready to act.
Inspire us and all those in the area
to do what we can, in your name,
to take responsibility, as your Son did,
in extending your love to those in need and distress.
Amen

385 Heavenly Father,
we need your strength today
as well as urgency and patience,
in the face of the disaster in . . .
Let the world you created respond,
individually and collectively,
generously and creatively,
to the challenge that faces local communities.
May the worldwide community see it as our responsibility
to help our neighbours as ourselves,
to take comfort from your presence in the midst of suffering
and to direct the skills and resources
where they are really needed,
loving Lord.
Amen

Flora and fauna

386 God of abundance,
you bring the rains and the sun
for the benefit of plants and animals,
as well as for our delight.
May their growth be blessed
and their needs met,

without let or hindrance from us,
but with our careful stewardship
of water and irrigation;
of solar and hydro-electric power;
of good gardening and responsible harvesting.
We ask this in your Son's name, Jesus Christ.
Amen

387 Lord of light and heat,
let all the creatures and plant life
be blessed in the world of your creation.
Let us not take for granted
that year after year,
hot summer after hard winter,
life begins again in the year's rotation.
Let us give thanks for this
and give a helping hand to nature
in our tending of plants and nurturing of animals.
May we have green fingers and tender hands
as we look after the natural world
that you have given us and which we must pass on,
Lord of nature and nurture.
Amen

388 God of surprise and joy,
may we rejoice in the abundance of flowers
in all sorts of surprising places.
And may we glory in the variety of wildlife,
even in places we may never go.
May we keep our distance
and give space to animals and humans alike,
and encourage plant life to flourish,
in gardens and wild places alike.
Keep endangered species safe from harm
and give rare plants a chance to thrive.
We ask this through your Son, Jesus Christ.
Amen

389 Gracious God,
who has given us the space and environment
to grow as you would want,
let us not be selfish in our use of your gifts.
Create in us the will and desire
to regard your creatures as our neighbours
and your plant life as our vineyard.
In enjoying your water and your wine,
let us acknowledge that without you
there would be no bread of life,
no living water,
no nourishment,
for our faith, our families, our future,
God of life-giving force.
Amen

Animals and pets

390 Loving Lord,
we thank you for the creatures of your world,
domesticated or wild, large and small.
Help us to treat them well,
as they are our neighbours too,
reminding us of the cycle of life
and the consequences of mortality.
Bring out the best in us
as we care for our animals and pets,
we pray.
Amen

391 God of companionship,
what a friend we have in Jesus,
born in a stable shared with animals,
showing care and concern for them
in life and in death.
Help us to model good practice
in animal husbandry,
so that we can look your Son in the face
in giving an account of ourselves.
Amen

392 Lord of land and sea,
may the creatures of your world
live in harmony with humankind,
bringing out the best in us
and nurturing the animal kingdom.
Set our standards high
so that we may give a good example
to our families, to our fellow humans,
and to future generations.
Amen

393 Lord of love,
may we show in our love of pets
a special bond between us and the rest of your creation,
in the knowledge that we are all one
in sharing the benefits of life,
the environment and your world.
We thank you for the special place of pets
in our lives and in our hearts.
Amen

394 God of creation,
we ask for your blessings on the animal kingdom,
for the joy that animals give us,
for the food that they provide,
for the milk and wool they offer us.
And when we plan our way of life
or changes in our environment,
help us to think carefully about
the impact of our actions
on the fauna and flora around us,
and pause (for prayer and thought) . . .
Amen

Death of a pet

395 Dear Lord,
we thank you for the life of a very special pet.
We are sorry that . . . is no longer with us,
but pleased that *he/she* is now with you.
We remember all the fun that . . . gave us.
It is always difficult to lose anyone or anything we love,
but we will always have our memories
to comfort us and offer to you,
through your Son, our friend, Jesus Christ.
Amen

Hot and cold

396 God of heat and light,
give us an appreciation
of the warmth of a fire in winter
and the cool of shade in summer.
May those who live in hot climates
be blessed with sufficient rain;
and those who live in temperate areas
feel the sun on their face in between the cloud.
Thank you for all the benefits of heat and cold.
Amen

397 God of balance and exchange,
let us give thanks for contrasts:
for the blessings of warmth
and the refreshment of cold.
But let us be mindful of extremes,
which explorers have experienced
during centuries of pushing back the frontiers
of height and depth, of danger and difficulty.
May we always appreciate the efforts of others
who test boundaries for our comfort and safety.
Amen

398 Heavenly Father,
you brought us sunshine and rainfall,
but also the challenge of drought and flood.
You gave us snows and rivers,
but also the challenge of ice and avalanche.
You created desert and ice cap,
but also the challenge of thirst and frostbite.
Challenge us, change us, but keep us safe.
Amen

399 God our refuge,
stretch our comprehension of extremes,
so that we can truly appreciate
the gift of warmth, not the distress of burning,
the refreshment of cooling, not the danger of freezing.
Let us respond and be glad
in the balm and variety
of the temperatures you give us.
Amen

400 Maker of heaven and earth,
bringer of heat and cold,
we thank you for the preservation of life,
through the blend of heat and light,
of water and wind.
In all the changes and chances of life,
let us celebrate the sheer variety of your creation,
the great blessing that this world provides,
the essential goodness of your love.
Amen

A polar prayer

401 God of ice and snow,
may we seek to protect the frozen wastes,
where life is harsh but nature is at work.
Let us not trespass too far or too often
into the habitat of penguins or polar bears,

of albatross or orca whale.
Let the ecology of the Arctic and Antarctic,
so important for the rest of the world,
be cherished and protected
and explored only to safeguard your creative generosity
in giving us such riches,
in letting us have such glimpses
of your magical kingdom, planet Earth.
Amen

THE WORLD

Freedom and democracy

402 Beneficent Lord,
you gave us the freedom to decide and to act,
in accordance with or against your will.
May we have the strength to follow your way,
avoiding temptation to stray
and seeking your forgiveness when we do.
May we so order our affairs
that our freedom can be subject to both your will
and the best rule of law that humankind can devise,
a framework of personal liberty and mutual responsibility.
Amen

403 God of grace,
set our hearts and minds at rest,
in the knowledge of your love,
so that in all our doings
we may be fairly treated
and show justice and mercy to others,
as your Son taught us.
May we always know our limitations
as well as seek to explore our ambitions,
provided they are in accordance with your will.
Amen

404 God of judgement and justice,
help us to make your kingdom known
through all we do, individually and collectively.
May those in authority and power
seek only to advance the position of the poor and deprived,
serving those least able to help themselves.
Empower and enable the downtrodden
so that they can have the stake in your world
which you promised in your kingdom.
Amen

405 Ever-living Lord,
your freedom gives hope to all;
your love gives peace to all.
May we respond to your grace,
by giving rights and taking responsibility,
by honouring elections and using the vote,
and by respecting the authority of legitimate government,
as your Son did.
Amen

406 God of peace,
help us so to manage our affairs
that the rule of law equates to your will for us.
Give to those who govern
the humility to know when their time has come,
to seek re-election
or to step down.
May we learn the lesson of history,
that we get the leaders we deserve,
whereas we can never earn your love,
except by your grace.
Amen

Government

407 God of majesty,
grant those who govern us in this world
the wisdom to do so fairly,
the ability to do so with skill,
And the judgement to plan ahead,
while responding to immediate need.
Through your Son we have learnt
to render to Caesar what is Caesar's
and we honour you by showing allegiance to government,
while working for justice and peace,
as he did.
Amen

408 Lord of all,
we are ever grateful for the laws you have given us,
in their stark simplicity.
May we learn the lessons of history
in the way we govern and are governed.
May we elect the leaders we need
or we are destined to have the leaders we deserve.
Send people with commitment and integrity
to guard us in this world,
while you guide us to the next.
We pray for peoples oppressed by dictatorships
and ask that the flame of truth
leads to the warmth of reconciliation,
through your Son, Jesus Christ.
Amen

409 Heavenly Father,
bring to our government, local and national,
a renewed drive to empower rather than control,
to serve rather than be served,
and not to flaunt the trappings of status and position.
Let the example of your Son
be the model for our lives
in governing fairly
and obeying proper authority.
But always encourage the gift of prophecy,
today as much as in the age of the great prophets,
who foretold the coming of your Son,
Jesus Christ.
Amen

410 Almighty God,
you have given us the free will to choose you
and out of grace you have accepted us as your own.
May we learn to use that free will
in our daily round too,
to work for what we believe is right in the world,
to vote for those who have the vision
to bring peace, justice and prosperity to an ailing world.

But may we be very mindful
of the love your Son showed
for the marginalised and disenfranchised,
when we seek change in society,
when we elect our political representatives,
when we obey our laws – and yours, gracious God.
Amen

Authority

411 God of power and might,
your authority is absolute
– and so very generously applied.
Your laws are strict
– and your judgements merciful.
Your vengeance is great
– and your reconciliation lasting.
Through your Son you have made all things new.
And from his death on the cross your authority
is transformed through his resurrection
into a new mandate,
to love and be loved, as you love us.
Amen

412 Heavenly Father,
we are in awe of you,
yet yearn to know you better.
We thank you that your Son
has shown us a new side to your authority.
May our leaders and governors
learn from his example
in challenging and encouraging,
by example and vision,
through deeds as well as words,
so that we come to respect them,
as we respect the grace and sacrifice
of your only Son, Jesus Christ.
Amen

413 All seeing Lord,
we ask that as you survey your world
you build up the courage of those in authority
to do the right thing;
to know when enough is enough;
to learn from mistakes made;
and to listen to our concerns.
We ask for your blessings on all in authority.
May their judgement be good
and their word their bond.
We ask this through your Son,
whose mercy is without limit
and whose rule is without end.
Amen

414 Just and merciful Father,
we build up those in authority
– and bring them down if they fail.
Yet your way is always to forgive,
where repentance is sincere
and amendment of life is the outcome.
On a sea of trouble you calm the waters.
So may our leaders react in difficult times
and may all who honour you
treat those under their authority
with justice, with integrity, with mercy.
In the name of the one who loves as you love him,
Jesus Christ.
Amen

The Sovereign

415 God who reigns,
bestow your grace and wisdom
on our sovereign, *Queen Elizabeth*,
and all the Royal Family,
so that the responsibilities they have inherited
may be carried out in a way which honours you.

May the Queen's chaplains serve our Governor well
and may *Her* Majesty watch over
the state of the Church,
as well as the state of the nation,
with your Son as *her* guide.
We ask this through Jesus Christ.
Amen

416 Heavenly Father,
whose rule extends from this kingdom to the next,
bring your blessings on *Elizabeth, our Queen*,
her heirs and descendants,
so that she may guide *her* subjects well
in all matters spiritual and temporal:
governing your Church and bringing wisdom and experience
to the task of prime ministers and governments,
always ready to discern your will
and committed to serve you,
enabling *her* to serve *her* people well,
with the help of Jesus Christ, your Son, our Lord.
Amen

417 Almighty God,
who gives us the breath of life
and draws us to himself,
we pray for our Sovereign, *Queen Elizabeth*,
as she carries out *her* duties.
May she be blessed with the stamina and sensitivity
to respond to all those who seek *her* aid,
the great and the good,
the poor and the marginalised,
the healthy and the suffering,
the government and the governed.
May *she* be blessed with your grace,
supported by *her* people and drawn to you
when *she* seeks your counsel,
Mighty Counsellor.
Amen

418 God of power and majesty,
we ask for your protection and mercy
on our Sovereign, *Queen Elizabeth*,
and all the Royal Family.
Bring them insight and judgement
in all their duties and relationships.
And may our *Queen* show
that in *her* governing of your Church
and in *her* role as Head of State,
she shows the fruits of *her* love for you
and the guidance of *her* chaplains
as *she* seeks to be your servant
in serving us, with the help of your Son,
Jesus Christ.
Amen

Coronation

419 Sovereign Lord,
we pray for *Her/His* Majesty, King/Queen . . . as *s/he* is anointed before you.
May *his/her* rule be just and inclusive.
Bring *him/her* wisdom, judgement and mercy,
your peace in this land and Commonwealth,
and good health to all the royal family.
Amen

420 God of power and might,
on the coronation of King/Queen . . .
May *he/she* follow your ways
in overseeing *his/her* government and Commonwealth,
persevering in prayer,
and listening to your call
as our Sovereign, Defender of faith,
and Governor of the Church of England.
Amen

Politics

421 Lord of hearts and minds,
send down on politicians
the gift of wisdom and the humility of servants.
May they learn to challenge the status quo
but never to change for change's sake.
Teach them to hear as well as listen
and act at all times with integrity,
as your Son taught us.
Amen

422 Sovereign Lord,
there is always a tide in the affairs of humankind,
which takes us on or sets us back.
Help all who govern discern the pattern of that tide
and know how to ride the surf
and avoid the quicksand.
Amen

423 Lord of strategy and oversight,
assist those who seek election
and stay with them if they take power.
May they set their sights high
but keep their feet on the ground.
Guide them, encourage them,
but let them understand
when it is time to go.
Amen

424 Almighty God,
you showed us through your Son
that the art of politics
is not to confront or control,
but to question and reflect back,
to lead by example,
not to misuse power.
Grant our politicians the vision
to make a difference to people's lives
without thought for their own.
Amen

425 Heavenly Father,
look down on our different forms of democracy
with benign and generous oversight.
May we understand the sheer diversity of mechanisms
to ensure the election and maintenance
of a proper government
and a means for voting them out.
May there always be a way of rendering to Caesar what is Caesar's,
and to God what is God's.
Amen

War and peace

426 God of peace,
may we so hate war
that we go the extra mile for peace.
May the threat or rumour of war
concentrate the minds of politicians and armies
to pull back from confrontation
and give reconciliation a chance.
Amen

427 Lord of integrity and purpose,
may we stop war in its tracks
by honouring diversity,
not by forcing uniformity.
You made us all different,
so let us celebrate that difference.
May peace be the natural order,
not one imposed by force.
May we know that through your Son,
Jesus Christ.
Amen

428 Father God,
who makes all things new,
let peace break out in unlikely places,
by dint of brave words and courageous acts.
You have shown us over time
that miracles happen,
especially in the people and places
we least expect.
Surprise us, Lord.
Amen

429 God of transformation,
peace you gave to us,
peace you expect of us.
Commission us to banish war
by sharing peace,
by sharing you, in bread and wine,
in church and society.
Amen

430 Rewarding Lord,
let us not look to heaven to heal all ills,
when your kingdom extends to earth
and we have a job to do here.
May we follow you to the ends of the earth,
not to dominate or dictate,
but to be good stewards
of your world, your peace,
your answer to the dead end of unjust wars.
Amen

Election/referendum

431 God of inclusion and diversity,
in this election/referendum may heart, head and spirit be fully engaged.
Whatever the result may the outcome be met
with a renewed willingness and generosity of spirit,

to work as neighbours and friends in this part of your world,
without triumphalism or bitterness,
as your Son would wish.
Amen

At Council meetings

432 God of authority and justice,
we ask that the deliberations here
will truly reflect your will.
May all that is said be from deep conviction
and a desire to do the right thing.
May Council members be always mindful
of those who elected them
and those whom they serve.
Let disagreement bring new insights;
let challenge provide new answers;
let decisions be based on vision;
and may those who implement what is agreed here
be confident that proper consideration
has been given to the consequences.
In the name of the one whose sacrifice
restored our relationship with you,
Jesus Christ.
Amen

433 Heavenly Father,
you only wish for the best for the governance of our affairs.
Pour down on this Council your grace and wisdom
so that issues are explored fully,
people are listened to as well as heard,
and there is adequate understanding of the decisions and outcomes.
Bring healthy debate and proper scrutiny
to all that is said and done here.
And may those who disagree
have the consolation of free speech to make their views known.

We ask this through the one who respected authority,
in this world and the next,
your Son, Jesus Christ.
Amen

434 Lord God,
who rules with justice and mercy,
watch over our Council meeting.
Let judgement and discernment be evident
in all the discussions and in the decisions taken.
May principles be to the fore,
whatever the political viewpoint.
But also let reconciliation and fairness reign,
so that implementation and outcomes
are properly understood and scrupulously carried out.
May the Council show itself
as you would want, creative God.
Amen

435 Almighty God,
as we gather for the business of Council,
let us remember those the Council serves
and those who serve the Council.
May we always know the limitations,
as well as the powers, of this body.
In exercising the Council's responsibility,
grant to members the energy and commitment
to be true to your purpose for us,
so that we may be confident
in our accountability to the community,
to the town/city/district of . . . ,
and to you, who will judge us all.
Amen

Negotiation, peacemaking and reconciliation

436 Lord of all,
we pray for the trouble spots of the world today,
in particular . . . ,
where negotiations are currently taking place.
May all the parties involved enter these in good faith,
resolved to find a way forward rather than looking
for new stumbling blocks.
Inspire the leaders with insight and vision,
so that good can come out of brokenness,
as your Son, Jesus Christ, would want.
Amen

437 God of the future,
let those who negotiate for reductions in our
wastefulness know your will.
Reveal to us the real dangers of our impact on your world.
We pray especially for those involved in negotiations on:
trade . . .
environmental policies . . .
arms control . . .
nuclear proliferation . . .
climate change.
Bring to us all a better understanding of good stewardship
in our part of your universe.
Amen

438 Amazing God,
your power is boundless and restrained,
captured in creation – and in the stillness of deep waters.
We need that restraint just now in . . . .
May those who are fighting understand that they are
desecrating your world
by their violence and selfishness.
Help them to know that it is not exercising superior
power that shows true strength,

but the perseverance to seek peace which marks
the wisdom of righteousness.
Help . . . in its hour of need through the example of your
Son, Jesus Christ.
Amen

THE CHURCH

National Church

439 Heavenly Father,
give to your Church the faith and the firmness
to weather the storms of controversy,
by discerning your purpose for the people of God,
by sharing your word through ministry and mission
and by sharing your love with those of faith
and with those with none.
Pour down on your bishops and priests
the stamina and the inspiration
to maintain and sustain your presence in the world,
through the grace that you have shown
through your Son.
Amen

440 Lord God,
you have shown us through your Son
and in the work of the disciples,
the saints and your pilgrim people,
that your Church is a force in the world.
Let all your people know
that the responsibility is ours
to minister and to pray,
to bring wholeness and caring,
to lighten the burdens of others.
May the pastoral witness of the churches
snuff out the taunts and jibes
of those who see only structures
instead of Christ at work.
Shine the light of hope and the beacon of faith in the world,
empowering God.
Amen

441 Almighty God,
we pray for our Church leaders,
our archbishops and bishops,
and all who influence the future of the Church,
including those on Archbishops' Council and General Synod,

and those who serve on Bishops' Advisory Panels.
Create in them the capacity to grasp and resolve issues
and to discern your will in all they do.
May relationships between denominations and between faiths
be blessed with respect and affection
at both national and local levels,
to give reconciliation the best hope of success.
Amen

442 Lord and Father,
bless our Church and its leaders;
bless our priests and laity;
bless our buildings and communities.
In return, may we give our best efforts
to the development of your Church,
in maturity and in response to the world,
so that our personal prayers and preoccupations
can be given wider vision and clearer focus.
Stretch us, Lord, inside out,
upside down, every which way,
so that we can be tested
– and not found wanting, we pray.
Amen

Leadership and discipleship

443 Lord of leadership,
encourage all who try to be your disciples.
May we learn your ways by listening to your Son.
And may we see how his disciples were challenged,
but also were led by example,
and then passed on your word
through their pastoral ministry,
as well as their preaching and teaching.
Give us the right leaders,
so that we can be good disciples.
Amen

444 Heavenly Father,
be a beacon of hope
and a shining star;
a plumb-line
and a leading light.
From the day of your Son's birth
to his lonely agony on the cross,
to the resurrection and ascension,
we were never let down,
unlike you,
never abandoned, unlike him.
Lead us, Heavenly Father,
to the ends of the earth – and beyond.
Amen

445 Amazing Lord,
God of justice and power,
let your will prevail
through love and relationship.
Let your love bring us through
and your Holy Spirit guide us on our way.
May we never let a stone stay unturned
in our efforts to share your love with others,
before you welcome us home.
Amen

446 God of mission,
send us out in your name:
to be good disciples;
to show true leadership;
to be good learners as well as teachers;
to wrestle with you,
and with each other,
if it brings us to see the truth,
the way and the life
that your Son gave us.
Amen

447 Lord of all,
make us and break us,
take us and remake us,
in your image,
in our imagination,
in our action,
and in our person.
Let your Holy Spirit work on us,
let your Son shape us,
and may you judge us.
Amen

Ecumenism

448 Lord of all,
let the fellowship of all believers
break through suspicions of different traditions.
Give to each denomination the will and the means
to confer together, work together
and subsume their distinctiveness
in the great mission of extending your kingdom.
May churches together
be greater than the sum of their parts,
for the sake of your Son, Jesus Christ.
Amen

449 Universal God, Heavenly Father,
you give to your people the freedom
to choose or reject you.
You have also seen your Church
divide and merge, struggle and unite.
In all this, may humankind's influence
be put aside in church matters,
so that denominations can see
what is common to us all
and how little we differ
in love for you,

in love of neighbour,
in response to need,
and in advancing your kingdom.
Amen

450 Almighty God,
who wants the best for us,
help us to give our best to you,
not just in worship
but in our daily round.
And let us join together
on the feast days and great festivals
to join our voices and forces
in praise of you,
as we seek a glimpse of you
in your great mission to us,
your Son, Jesus Christ.
Amen

451 God of harmony and purpose,
may we come to grow in ecumenical co-operation
in our community,
in our land,
and across the worldwide Church.
Your Son showed us the right path,
yet we have strayed down blind alleys,
as well as highways and byways,
ostensibly in search of you,
but often to meet our own goals.
Create in us, we pray,
the compass we need
to have a right relationship with you,
forgiving and patient Lord.
Amen

Relationship to other faiths

452 God of all,
let us continue to discern the one true way,
while recognising that others are still on a journey.
May we not presume to map their route to you,
so help us to be sensitive in our mission to them,
not disguising our faith,
but never assuming our superior knowledge.
May all those of faith be guided by you, our beacon,
and through your Son, our compass.
Amen

453 Creator God,
bring us gently onto the true path,
through revelation,
through explanation, through exploration.
But let us honour those on different paths,
praying that we all converge on you.
Let us not be sidetracked by condemning those others,
but help us to model your Son's way,
challenging, asking for and practising
your Son's love for humankind.
Amen

454 Lord God,
you uphold the faith that sustains us,
even in the darkest moments.
May others feel that same love,
even if it has been revealed to them in different ways.
Give to all those of faith a special place in your heart,
shown in the compassion of your Son,
as he demonstrated your way.
Amen

455 Father God,
in the midst of joy or sadness,
may we call on the strength of your presence,
to share that happiness or despair.

And may those of different faiths,
and those in search of truth,
see in our response
a glimpse of what can be
and a shared moment of unity,
with us and with you,
universal God.
Amen

456 Trusting Lord,
you empower us with the Spirit
to learn your ways and heed your call.
In your Son's mission to humankind
he welcomed Gentiles and Samaritans
to share the feast of your heavenly kingdom.
May we, in our dealings with people of different faiths,
remember the mission of your disciples,
who ensured that the faith survived.
Equip us to express mission today
in fresh ways, in creative ways,
in love.
Amen

457 God of power and might,
bless all who confess their faith
through revelation, upbringing, culture or teaching.
We count our blessings as Christians
that you have shown us the way,
the truth and the light
through your Son's incarnation
and our salvation through the cross.
May those of other faiths respect ours
and may we as Christians
show hospitality and generosity
in our relationship with them.
Give us broad shoulders
and faithful hearts.
Amen

458 Immanent God,
let all the nations know your name
and may all peoples feel your love.
Give to people of all faiths and none
the opportunity to turn to you,
helped by our witness, our openness
and our respect for neighbour and friend,
stranger and traveller.
May we seek to understand those of different faiths,
as every person is precious in your eyes.
We ask for the insight of your Holy Spirit
so that we can relate to all your creation.
Amen

459 God of difference and inclusion,
your Son related to Jew and Gentile,
to sinner and Samaritan,
to publican and prostitute,
to tax collector and outcast.
May we be as inclusive and open,
not only to individuals
but also to other faiths,
even when we are the object of antagonism.
Help us to be open to learn through exposure to challenge,
and may we be inspired
by the saints and martyrs down the ages,
with the help of your Son, Jesus Christ.
Amen

460 Loving Lord,
you are forever young –
and timeless too.
Have mercy on all in this life
as we come and go.
May the love that you have for us
be felt by all who turn to you.
Help us to witness to that love in our own lives
so that, by your grace,
people of other faiths may be drawn to you
and our differences be seen in perspective,
God of time and space.
Amen

Diocese, deanery and parish

461 Lord God,
we give thanks for our church
and this your congregation.
Bring us insight and inspiration
so that we can know your presence
and worship your majesty.
But help us also to reach out to our neighbouring churches,
learning from them and listening to them,
showing and sharing their fellowship
and joining together on mission projects
in our community and beyond.
May our focus be local
but our vision much wider,
as your Son's was.
Amen

462 Almighty God,
make us, your people, your true servants,
not only in church but also in community.
May we welcome people in
and may they feel your Holy Spirit in this place.
Give to those who minister here
and all who worship your name
the confidence to pray in hope
and the means to do your will.
Let us be a church which loves you
and a church where you are teaching us
to be more like your Son,
our Saviour, Jesus Christ.
Amen

463 God of beauty and might,
look down on our worshipping community,
and on our church, with grace and with mercy.
Heal us when we suffer.
Challenge us when we are content.
Bring us to an understanding of our neighbours

as we understand more about you.
And may we see Jesus
in all that we attempt here,
in our worship and praise
and in our mission and ministry.
May we always feel your presence
– and rejoice.
Amen

464 Lord of great things and small things,
you know the value of each person
and make us all feel special.
May every church make a difference,
every prayer matter,
and every kindness show your love.
Let our church be a place
where all are welcome,
visitor, stranger, young, old,
and where you are present
in all our actions and activities,
in our busyness and in your peace.
Help us to look forwards and look up,
even when we are deeply in prayer,
for your Son's sake.
Amen

At parochial church councils

465 Almighty God,
be with us in our deliberations
as we seek to discern your will
for our church and congregation.
May we listen more than speak,
reflect before we decide,
and always consider how our decisions
may advance your kingdom.
Give us insight and wisdom
and the commitment to see things through.
Amen

466 Heavenly Father,
bring to our meeting clarity and purpose,
the willingness to do things properly,
but also to take risks for you.
Fill our discussions with your Holy Spirit,
so that we keep to your grand design
and make decisions which shape our mission
and reflect your will.
And may we be good listeners,
to each other and to you;
we ask in Jesus' name.
Amen

467 Father of all,
we ask for your presence with us now
in our deliberations and debate.
May we disagree in love
and compromise with generosity,
always drawing on the principles
your Son shared with us.
So help us to foresee the impact of our decisions
on the poor and the weak
as well as the rich and strong;
on the visitor and stranger
as well as the regular attender.
Give us insight and judgement,
we pray, as we begin our meeting.
Amen

468 Lord God,
help us as we meet to focus on what you would want of us.
Make this a time for prayer in action,
working your purpose out together, in fellowship.
Bring us a sense of responsibility to others and to you;
bring us a sense of excitement as we confer about the future;
bring us a sense of what has gone before,
so that we can build on firm foundations of faith,
of service, of love.
Amen

At synods

469 Almighty God,
grant to your synod wisdom in our proceedings,
a desire to extend your kingdom,
and the ability to choose the right priorities.
We value the gift of debate
and honour the right to disagree.
But may all that we do
be according to your will
for the good of your Church.
Amen

470 God of hope,
may the issues before us at this synod
be viewed through the prism of Christian love.
Let us voice and examine every concern
as we seek to discern the best ways forward.
Give us the courage to challenge,
and if necessary change, our structures
in order that we may show
that your kingdom comes first
in our procedures as in our lives.
Amen

471 Lord God,
you have given us the freedom to choose.
May there be freedom of debate today
within the bounds of respect and propriety.
May we seek to shape policy and practice
to meet the needs of both maintenance and mission,
using the precious gift of finance
to support and extend the ministry of your Church
in a world of spiritual deprivation and need.
Amen

472 Father of all,
as your Church seeks to withstand the forces of secularism,
may we feel empowered and emboldened,
by your Holy Spirit, to implement your agenda
rather than respond to the agenda of others.
Strengthen our vision for the future of our diocese *(deanery)*
and bring forward people of quality to do your work
in our parishes and deaneries,
in our churches and communities,
with the help of your Son, Jesus Christ.
Amen

A prayer for treasurers

473 God of great gifts and great mercies,
watch over all treasurers and those who administer money
on behalf of others.
May they always be true to your purpose,
guide others in the proper use of funds,
and be fearless in the face of misuse of money.
Let their ministry be acknowledged and their counsel heeded,
especially where there are disputes and discord.
May we all share in the task they have,
through our support and concern,
by our prayers and deeds.
We ask this in Jesus' name.
Amen

A prayer for a church legacy group

474 Lord of life and legacy,
we ask for your blessing on this meeting
as we wrestle with the best ways to honour your name
and the wishes of those who are now with you,
in your heavenly kingdom.
Let us be aware of the needs of the church today,
but also take decisions that will bring lasting enhancement

to the place were we worship,
and future generations will worship,
(name of church),
so that it is both our church and your Church.
Amen

Baptism

475 Dear Lord,
please welcome . . . to your Church today.
With water your Son was baptised by John.
With water . . . is made a member of our congregation.
May all in the family and the church family celebrate this special day:
special for . . . ,
special for *his/her* parents,
special for *his/her* godparents,
and special for you, loving Father,
as the continuity of your kingdom
takes another step forward,
another opportunity for Christian hope,
another blessing, through your Son, our Saviour,
Jesus Christ.
Amen

476 Heavenly Father,
we are taking this step . . .
knowing that you want to welcome *him/her*
to your Church.
Help us to be good parents and wise counsellors.
Let the light of Christ shine in . . . *'s* life,
and whatever challenges *he/she* may face,
we pray that you are always alongside,
ready to lift and protect, as well as encourage and enable.
Thank you for the next phase in *his/her* life,
which we celebrate in Jesus' name.
Amen

477 God of new beginnings,
I ask that this step I am taking to be baptised
is one which you wish me to take.
It is not easy for me, at my age,
to seek to make up for lost time.
But I really want to be a full member of your Church,
to be blessed with water in the name of Father, Son,
and Holy Spirit,
to experience even more closely the love
that you have already shown,
the compassion that I feel as I get to know your Son.
Help me through this transition and strengthen me
in the faith,
through Jesus Christ.
Amen

478 Almighty God,
our church today rejoices in celebration,
as . . . is welcomed as a pilgrim on the
Christian way.
May the water and the sign of the cross
mark the start of . . . *'s* journey,
and may the light of Christ illuminate *his/her* path,
so that as *he/she* takes *his/her* first steps and grows in
strength and independence,
he/she may feel your love grow into faith that lasts.
We ask this through Jesus Christ, our Lord.
Amen

479 Gracious Lord,
let me take very seriously the task of being a godparent,
knowing that I have been entrusted with important
responsibilities.
Help me to recall the ways in which my godparent*(s)*
assisted me,
and let me remember how I felt about it.
More than anything, Lord, let me do your will in all
I attempt,
and may . . . *'s* spiritual well-being be a prime focus.

If I can show a fraction of your Son's love for me,
I'll be doing a good job.
Through the one who shows us the way, now and always,
Jesus Christ.
Amen

Confirmation

480 Entrusting God,
you received me at my baptism,
and gave responsibility to my parents and godparents
to bring me up in the faith of Christ.
Now I want to take my own step on that journey
as I seek your blessing on my confirmation.
In all this you have been my compass and my shield.
As I travel further on your path,
let me be always open to the Holy Spirit
and ready to play a full part in our Christian community.
We ask this in Jesus' name.
Amen

481 Lord of spirit and grace,
come down on . . . today.
Release and confirm *him/her* in *his/her* faith,
so that *he/she* may grow in the love of your Son
and make that personal connection with you
that will last throughout this life and into the next.
In silence and in confidence we pray for . . .
and all others being confirmed today.
Knowing that you listen to our prayers
and see into our hearts,
come close through your Son, Jesus Christ.
Amen

482 God our guide and our compass,
as . . . confirms *his/her* Christian commitment,
let us all – family and friends, parents and godparents –
support and encourage *him/her* on the path your Son

taught us,
whatever the temptations to stray.
Bring purpose to *his/her* life
and a willingness and burning desire
to know you better and make you better known,
through the love of your Son, Jesus Christ.
Amen

483 God of growth,
today is all about sharing the light of Christ
as . . . takes the next step in faith.
Illuminate the way and shine even in dark corners,
so that *he/she* can be a witness to the love
that you have bestowed.
We give thanks for the job of godparents,
who are always there to bring a special contribution,
encouraging the nurturing of *his/her* spiritual side.
In the midst of everything else expected nowadays,
bring a sacred space to *his/her* heart
and a love of community to *his/her* worship,
through the one who shared everything, Jesus Christ.
Amen

484 Almighty God,
you have given us the gift of life.
You have also provided us with insight and free will
to make up our minds and develop our beliefs.
Assist the transition that those who are being confirmed
are making.
It is just one step along the way,
but a big one, Lord.
Just as you have been with people in their first,
faltering steps of faith,
enveloped in the love that baptism brought,
so now protect and grow their faith
in order to bring you nearer.
Thank you, Lord.
Amen

485 Almighty God,
as the faith of . . . is confirmed we ask that *he* is upheld
and supported in *his* beliefs by all present today.
May this significant milestone in *his* faith journey
be a source of inspiration for *him* and a creative
opportunity for the church.
We pray that through your grace and *his* faith,
his life may be strengthened and your kingdom extended.
We ask this through Jesus Christ, our Lord.
Amen

486 Almighty God,
we pray for those being confirmed today.
May your high expectations, Lord, be matched by their
faithfulness.
On this special occasion, when their baptism is transformed
into confirmation by your grace and their free will, let this
church rejoice and their school(s) applaud.
May the sacraments deepen their spiritual experience of you
and encourage them in the exploration of their faith.
In a moment's silence let us pray for the individual(s) being
confirmed . . .
Let us pledge ourselves to doing all we can to support them
in their commitment.
We ask this through Jesus Christ, our Lord.
Amen

487 Affirming Lord,
grant to your candidate(s) the openness to grow in faith,
so that your Holy Spirit shows itself
in action and word,
in sacrament and prayer,
in repentance and forgiveness.
May the sharing of the bread and the wine
be seen as a blessing and a symbol
of the body and blood of your Son.
And may every Eucharist
be a thanksgiving and a self-giving,
a breaking and a shedding,
but unifying us in you,
through your Son, Jesus Christ.
Amen

488 God of trust and empowerment,
launch your candidate(s) onto the sea of faith,
sure of their navigation,
always looking to the stars,
relying on their compasses along the way,
and trusting in your support in rough seas.
Give to all those keen to know you better
the gift of exploring and deepening their faith,
so that they can glimpse the mind of God,
through the taking of the wine and the bread,
as a timeless reminder of the sacrifices your Son suffered,
not just for humankind as a whole,
but for you and me.
Amen

489 Forgiving, giving God,
take your candidate(s) into the heart and soul of faith,
so that in receiving the bread and the wine
they may see the bread as your Son's body, broken for us,
and may know the wine as your Son's blood, shed for us.
May the mystery of faith become clearer,
so that hearts are warmed with your Holy Spirit,
and minds are filled with the wonder of understanding
of a wisdom born of knowledge,
but matured in relationship
with your Son, our Saviour, Jesus Christ.
Amen

490 Lord of light,
awaken in your servant(s)
a growing sense of you in their heads;
a desire to know the Holy Spirit in their faith journey;
a wonder at your creation in their eyes;
a love for their neighbours in their actions;
a knowledge of your presence in the breaking of the bread;
an appreciation of your Son's sacrifice in the sharing of the wine.
And may they walk in your ways
as long as they live,
faithful Father, loving Lord.
Amen

Weddings

491 God of union and unity,
may . . . and . . . know your love,
as they share all they are and all they have.
Let them be what you want them to be,
growing in mutual respect,
searching for truth, and finding
    the extraordinary in the ordinary;
    trust amidst the trials;
    an epiphany in the unexpected.
And may the wonder of their love never cease,
in their hearts and throughout their lives.
Amen

492 Lord of life and love,
pour down your blessings on . . . and . . . .
May they grow in understanding and trust as they embark on their future life together. May the bonds that unite them be strong enough to resist the temptations to stray. And may they be all the stronger for the love and affection from all around on this wedding day. Give them the heart and soul to show, in their love for one another, a selflessness and caring concern which shine out as a beacon of hope and a reflection of your love for them, gracious God.
Amen

493 Bringer of peace and love,
we pray for couples approaching their wedding day, for the careful preparation of practical arrangements, but also in getting ready for the emotional and spiritual challenges that the day itself will bring.
Give patience and perseverance to all concerned and make the whole experience of the wedding worthy of the occasion,
worthy of you, Lord,
and special in the eyes of all who attend. May wedding days be feast days for all involved – and for you too, Lord, God of purpose and destiny.
Amen

494 Father of all,
your love stretches to your whole creation, yet also to each individual family.
Grant . . . and . . . the favour of your presence, in their love, in their lives, on this special day.
Let the heavens rejoice with you
to see these two pledge their faithfulness
to each other, to the solemn vows of marriage and to a future together, under your protection.
Give them the strength to persevere
when times get tough
and the time and space together
to get to know each other day by day, in the hope of Christ.
Amen

495 Heavenly Father,
we gather to witness the union of . . . and . . .
before you, before the world, in the midst of shared love,
and in the shining light of your approval.
May they gain the knowledge of the hope and inspiration
that comes from a true appreciation
of the holy state of matrimony,
the highs and lows of life together, the prospect of children,
if that is your will, Lord,
and, above all, the gift of sharing, the wonder of love,
and the promise of your presence whenever they need the reassurance and reconciliation of your Son, Jesus Christ.
Amen

A prayer for Back to Church Sunday

496 We ask for your blessings on this Back to Church Sunday:
on those who have stepped over the threshold of church
for the first time in a while;
on those who are trying church for the first time;
and on those who have invited people to join us today.
May our welcome be your welcome;
may our joy be your joy;

and may the life of your Church
keep up with your search for new ways
to find us, to teach us, and to love us.
Amen

Prayers for an interregnum

497 Lord of beginnings and endings, first and last,
as we give thanks for the ministry of . . .
help us to look forward,
in hope and expectation,
and to discern your will
in the search for a new *vicar/priest/minister.*
Amen

498 Provider God,
you have given us good gifts
to use wisely and well.
Help us in our efforts
to find the person you have chosen
to be our next vicar/priest/minister.
May we work together for this one purpose
and seek to do our best to minister to your people
during the interregnum,
with your Holy Spirit as our helper.
Amen

499 Almighty God,
you know our ways,
our strengths and our weaknesses.
Give us the gifts of discernment and co-operation
in the task you have set before us
as we continue our work in your Church,
persevering in prayer and ministering to all,
in the sure and certain hope
of the right appointment and a new beginning.
Amen

500 Lord of continuity and change,
guide us in the months ahead,
in preparation and contemplation,
in advertising and interviewing,
in selection and appointment;
and in calling on help with ministering to the *parish/benefice.*
May we always, first and last,
look to you for discernment and inspiration,
in the process of decision-making
and in the welcome and induction of your new minister
among us.
Amen

INCLUSION AND DIVERSITY

Ethnicity

501 God of great diversity,
let us rejoice in the differences in your world,
symbolised in cultures and races.
May we all have pride in our own ethnicity,
while respecting that of others,
in our country and abroad,
in our places of worship
and in our communities.
Amen

502 Lord of Jew and Gentile,
your Son taught us how to expect the best of others,
irrespective of race, class or gender.
We remember how he was rejected as the Messiah of the Jews,
yet brought salvation to us all.
Samaritans, tax collectors, Canaanite women:
all were brought to him by faith,
and he reciprocated by welcoming them
into his kingdom, your kingdom, our kingdom.
Amen

503 Serene and sensitive Lord,
you send us out in your name,
to explore your will in all its diversity.
Open our eyes to the delights of difference,
showing us how ethnicities can unite
as well as divide our world.
May Christ our cornerstone
be the uniting factor
in supporting the span of humankind
in your world, our home.
Amen

504 Great and glorious King of kings,
your empire embraces all creeds, colours and cultures.
May we see the best in each other
under your rule.

May we show the best of ourselves
in honouring the difference.
May we share the best of your love
in our dealings with others.
Let us not cry for our beloved country,
but laugh with joy at its richness.
Amen

505 Sovereign Lord,
let us search out our feelings
about other ethnicities.
Let us reflect on how those feelings
have changed;
need to change;
are affected by our faith.
Help us to be honest, open, and true,
to ourselves, to others, and, above all,
to the one who has taught us
how to love our neighbour as ourselves,
Jesus Christ.
Amen

Religion

506 Gracious God,
you taught us how to love you
by sending your Son to be alongside us.
In all the mystery and majesty of your word,
may we never forget
the origins of that creation
begun, continued and extended in you.
Your Son has brought us close,
but let us bridge that short gap
between us and eternity,
by turning to the one who brings us
the peace of God which passes all understanding,
your Son, our Saviour,
Jesus Christ.
Amen

507 Lord,
it sometimes seems that there is too much religion in the world
and not enough faith.
Yet in religion you have given us the capacity
to worship you reverently and joyfully,
knowing that you hear our prayer
and receive our praise.
Help us to be
a bit more faithful in our religion,
a bit less religious in our faith.
Amen

508 Almighty God,
you give us the opportunity and the desire to worship you.
Let us not only feel the need to do so,
but the desire to show our love and praise.
In choosing to follow your Son,
we do so with joy in our heart.
In trusting you, let us respect
the hope that others have also,
even though they may express that faith in different ways.
Amen

509 God of power and might,
we acknowledge you to be our king.
Bring us greater knowledge and understanding of your kingdom
and also of the rival claims to that kingdom.
Through our faith, let us open doors rather than close them;
through your promises, let us be tested and not found wanting.
Strengthen us in our faith
and stretch us to express that faith in fresh ways.
Amen

510 Lord of all,
build in us the blessings of baptism;
create in us the confidence of confirmation;
equip us to engage in evangelism;
and never let us stray
from being partners in your mission,
to humankind, neighbour and friend,
stranger and outcast, young and old.
Amen

Atheists and agnostics

511 God of knowledge and understanding,
you let us all decide
whether to seek you out
and whether to keep on looking
when we search in the wrong places.
May we have the will to continue to explore,
but may we also spare a thought and a prayer
for those who have given up,
for those who never started,
and for those who have rejected you,
even though you have never rejected them.
Amen

512 God of hope,
even when the field is apparently lost,
all is not lost;
even when hope is seemingly gone,
faith is waiting to be found.
Bring us hope, Jehovah,
bring us love, Lord God,
and may those who don't believe
never give up the possibility of your presence.
If they think there is probably no God,
it means there possibly is,
and with you all things are possible,
merciful Lord.
Amen

513 Lord of love,
may atheists and agnostics have their say,
without attracting our alarm or anger.
But may atheists and agnostics
also acknowledge our right to believe,
whatever our denomination or faith.
You are far too important
for us to tick off or cross out
as a lifestyle option or an accepted fact.
People have fought and died for you,
so religion deserves challenge
as well as respect,
exploration rather than blind obedience.
Amen

514 Lord God,
help us to understand
that knowing you is loving you;
that not knowing you is depriving you of love,
but not stopping your love for us.
Give us time to grow
and time to know.
And may you never give up on us,
as you showed through your Son,
our Saviour, Jesus Christ.
Amen

515 God of grandeur,
it sometimes seems that you are too great to ignore,
yet still people do – and we occasionally do too.
Give courage to those with belief
to admit to moments of doubt.
But let atheists see that they can doubt too,
and may agnostics recognise the creativity of doubt,
so that sparks of belief can ignite the embers of faith,
to your glory – and theirs too.
Amen

Gender

516 God of love,
you have given us male and female
to bring us companionship,
to bring us children,
to bring happiness and joy.
But we ask for your healing hand
upon clashes and difficulties between men and women,
upon misunderstandings which get out of hand,
and upon the bereaved in their loss of a loved one.
Be our companion and guide,
in good times and bad.
Amen

517 Creator God,
may gender be a reason to rejoice,
not a reason to judge.
We ask for your blessings
on all who are unsure of their gender,
that there may be understanding and respect
for differences and confusion.
And may the battle of the sexes
be reserved for the theatre and film,
rather than the home and the hearth.
Amen

518 Gracious God,
'vive la différence' we say,
and for which we give you thanks.
In all our lives
we are blessed, challenged and affected
by relationships across genders and
from birth to death;
from love to hate;
from hurt to health.
May we experience the richness of those relationships
and learn from mistakes made.
Amen

519 Inclusive God,
may those who relate more to their own gender
be able to share and show their love
without judgement or accusation.
Let loyalty and fidelity be the true mark of love,
and the real test, in life as in our faith,
as you showed in remaining loyal to us,
even when we turned our back on you,
forgiving Lord.
Amen

520 Lord of life,
set our sights high in seeking and showing love.
Let us learn from your Son the need
to listen
to enquire
to teach
to challenge
to forgive.
But not
to judge
to ignore
to dismiss
to fight back
to betray.
Be a kind teacher for a hard task.
Amen

Sexuality

521 God of the senses,
we thank you for the delights of making love,
for the feelings you have given us,
as well as the means to express them.
We have been given these gifts
to use wisely and well,
though sometimes with abandon.
Let us rejoice and be glad.
Amen

522 Heavenly Father,
look down with favour on those you have created,
the diversity and difference,
as well as the common bonds of humanity.
May the joys of sexual attraction
be directed aright,
not just according to human rules,
but by your divine guidance,
so that we can honour
the fruits of your creation,
even when the norms of humankind are broken.
Amen

523 Great God of hope,
may our sexual encounters
be full of your grace.
May our lives fulfil expectations
and confound experience.
May we learn from loss
and value faithfulness.
Let our relationships reflect our faith,
in our desire to be worthy of you
in our honouring of partners.
Amen

524 Lord God,
we rejoice in our sexuality,
whatever our preferences.
Help us to be true to ourselves,
but remain true to you.
In our community, at work and at home,
let us choose our lifestyle carefully,
and honour our partners faithfully.
Bring good out of our relationships
and help us not to hurt or be hurt.
Amen

525 Lord of lords,
we are your unworthy servants,
but make us worthy of your love,
not only in our prayers and praise,
but in our lives,
the way we love,
the way we trust,
the way we work,
the way we are,
the way we thank you,
through Jesus Christ, our Lord.
Amen

Disability

526 God of strength and weakness,
you showed your vulnerability
through your Son's mission to earth,
his acceptance of suffering,
his openness to the needs of others.
May his example to the rich and able,
and his reaching out to the meek and the lame,
give heart to all,
challenging the strong and uplifting the weak.
Amen

527 God of triumph and tragedy,
may we all see a glass half full,
in counting our blessings
and knowing our gifts.
May we seek to make the most of those gifts
and take our social needs in our stride.
May our impairments make us stronger
and our disabilities spur us to overcome them,
by perseverance, by determination,
and by your grace.
Amen

528 Enabling Lord,
send us out in the power of your Spirit
to live, to work, to play and to love
without self-consciousness or fear.
Let our frailties draw on your strength
and our strength inspire others.
Let us be a community of enablers,
gracious Lord.
Amen

529 God of hope,
bring to us all your Son's inclusive words,
in inviting all to join him
in a kingdom free of prejudice.
Bring to us his inclusive heart,
in bringing your word to Jew and Gentile,
rich and poor, able-bodied and disabled.
May we all learn from those in need
and give in return our time as much as our resources.
Amen

530 Lord of all time,
lift up hearts and spirits
when misfortune strikes.
Bring wholeness in place of emptiness
when despair takes over.
Bring healing to ailments
when faith is evident.
May disabilities be transformed
into strength of spirit
which overcomes all and inspires many.
Amen

Height and weight

531 Almighty God,
your Son experienced the highs and lows of mortal life;
let our lives be richer for his sacrifice

high on the cross, borne down by his own weight,
but redeeming us all by his precious blood.
Let us be sensitive to the significance
of height and weight,
in our lives,
in giving you thanks.
Amen

532 Heavenly Father,
you have made us all shapes and sizes,
part of life's rich pattern and diversity.
But never let us think
that by being tall or short,
fat or slim, heavy or lightweight,
we are somehow better or inferior.
Judge us, Lord, by our spirit,
our faith and our works,
as we seek to be part of your kingdom.
Amen

533 Lord of gifts and gaps,
may we be long on patience;
let us be short with pomposity.
May we be great on prayer;
let us be miserly on anger.
May we be weighed down with generosity;
let us be light on seriousness.
Give us the mystery of a miracle
and the depth of a parable.
Amen

534 God of greatness,
may we strive to know the extent of your greatness,
without ever really knowing.
May we seek the depth of your wisdom,
without fully comprehending.
Give us a glimpse of eternity
without revealing all,
until we meet in your kingdom,
face to face.
Amen

535 Lord of great weight,
we know that we can never see infinity,
just as we can never understand eternity.
But in our appreciation of height and weight,
never let us lose sight of the essence
of mind and matter,
of personality and character,
rather than seeking to measure or weigh them.
Amen

Age

536 Lord of all the years,
let time be our friend, not our enemy.
Help us to grow up safely,
grow old gracefully,
and always grow in faith and understanding of you.
You gave us Old Testament and New,
so that we might fully appreciate
the lengths to which you have gone
to save us from ourselves and for you,
through your Son, Jesus Christ.
Amen

537 Ageless God,
who has been since before time,
who created where there was nothing,
and who will be forever,
look down on our world
and reclaim it as yours,
through the actions and teaching
of your Son's disciples through the ages,
stemming from your intervention in the world,
through your Son, our Saviour,
Jesus Christ.
Amen

538 God of grand designs,
when you gave us the world,
you did not leave it ticking by itself,
unchecking clock-like laws.
We give thanks for your constant watch
over the varied futures of your people,
our waywardness and faithfulness,
our disobedience and discipleship.
We thank you that you did not give up on us.
Amen

539 Sovereign Lord,
give us hope down all our years,
so that we can make sense of what has gone
and prepare for what will be.
May the vulnerability of childhood
become the energy of youth,
and the responsibility of parenthood
become the wisdom of age.
May the generations not always see eye to eye,
but may they always learn from one another.
Amen

540 God of memory and moment,
help us to have fond memories
of people and places we have known,
of our successes and failures,
of our lives and losses.
May age bring out the best of those memories,
and push to one side
the negativity and resentment,
forgiving but not forgetting
any hurt we may have suffered from others.
We ask this in the name
of the one who forgave and forgives,
Jesus Christ.
Amen

Wealth and poverty

541 Lord of creation,
you have given us infinite riches
in the cosmos and in our world.
Help us to appreciate that your resources
are for everyone, not just for a few.
Where we find unfairness,
may we seek to change it;
where we see hunger,
may we respond to need.
Let us be your agents
in sharing what we have
with those without their fair share
of what is yours.
Amen

542 God of the poor,
may we learn from the spirit of those with less
and not aspire to become those with more, at their expense.
Let us reach out,
not only with practical help,
but with joyful hearts.
Let us become partners in your enterprise
in linking humanity to each other and to you,
with the help of your Son,
Jesus Christ.
Amen

543 Lord of free will,
make us more aware of what we should do
to honour you with our heart and with our possessions.
Do we have to give away one to gain the other?
Or can we commit to you
as well as making our possessions work for you?
As we follow on from the young lawyer who asks your Son,
may we reflect and make the right choices in your sight.
Amen

544 Saving Lord,
let us know how best we can respond
to your generosity in creating our world and seeking your Son.
How can we ever repay you?
We pray for guidance
as we meet poverty;
as we see great wealth;
as we become aware of inequality;
as we experience overwhelming hospitality,
often from those with least.
Turn us upside down
in our expectations and in our responses.
Amen

545 Sovereign God,
when you bring us the days of wine and roses,
may we rejoice but also reflect,
so that we do not lose sight of the needs of the world.
May the wealth that we have
be directed at the poverty that is always with us,
not because of guilt and shame,
but because you have shown us the way to share,
to sacrifice,
to include rather than exclude.
Amen

COMMUNITY

Society

546 Merciful Father,
help us as Christians to play our full part
in our society and community,
both as individuals and as a church.
Your Son taught us not to set ourselves apart,
but to treat neighbour as self,
not to seek position or look down on others,
and to seek you in the poor and outcast.
Let the mission of our churches reflect these priorities,
engaging with society
and taking a prophetic role where necessary,
as witnesses to your will for us.
Amen

547 Caring Lord,
may we take our social responsibility seriously,
as Christians, as citizens, as your disciples.
Give us the desire and capacity
to serve you in serving others;
to challenge those who ignore the public good;
to champion the marginalised, the deprived, the oppressed;
and to share your hope in the love of Christ.
May your kingdom embrace our big society
with the inspiration of the Holy Spirit.
Amen

548 Heavenly Father,
pour down your blessings on the structures of our society.
May they work for those they serve,
not for the status or power of those in charge.
Help your Church to be an example and model,
working collaboratively and selflessly,
reaching out as your Son showed us,
empowering others to take responsibility
as your Son did,
and using the judgement and creativity
you have given us
to make a difference in your world.
Amen

549 Almighty God,
bring us better understanding and insight
as we seek transformation in society.
May our efforts prosper
if they are grounded in prayer, research and reflection.
Help us to take the necessary steps
to equip ourselves for the tasks ahead,
learning from others,
praying for courage and confidence,
and taking risks for you,
knowing that you will pick us up
as long as we have failed in good faith
rather than backed away in fear.
May we always ask what your Son would have done,
as the Church responds to problems in society.
Amen

Family and society

550 Father of all,
we rejoice in the joys of family.
May we seek always to develop our roles,
as child, parent, carer or relative,
so that we encourage relationship,
model faithfulness,
empower development,
and acknowledge weaknesses.
Give us discernment and humility
as our roles change,
over time and in love.
Amen

551 Enabler, Comforter,
give us insight, peace and love,
as we work out our relationships,
with you, with family, with friends.
May we give of ourselves
as we receive from others.

May we share our experience
where relevant and where needed.
May we keep our counsel
when we have nothing to add.
May we play our part,
in community, parish and network,
so that all benefit,
and no one is diminished.
Amen

552 Neighbour, friend, Lord,
may we see you in our street
and not walk by on the other side.
Help us to take responsibility
for our attitude to others.
Give us the skills and the will
to take our roles seriously,
but ourselves lightly,
always seeking to play our part
in reconciling, representing, recognising, rewarding,
so that good is acknowledged
and bad is resisted,
for the benefit of all,
but mostly for your sake.
Amen

553 Lord,
give us the confidence to take the reins,
as others fall by the wayside.
May our willingness to share others' burdens
lead to others helping us with ours.
As all things must pass,
so may all things come to fruition,
with all of us playing our part,
at home, at church, in society,
but only with you as our help,
our sole purpose,
and our reason to believe.
Amen

554 God of great things,
help us in the small things,
so that we can grow in hope.
Equip us to lead,
as well as follow.
Inspire us to teach
as well as learn.
May we be good disciples,
fruitful prayers,
loyal friends,
and good Samaritans,
wherever we go,
whoever we are,
in sickness and in health.
Amen

Local community

555 Lord of all,
bring us a real sense of community
in our villages and towns, our cities and suburbs.
And may that extend from our homes to our streets,
to our places of work and places of study.
May the God that draws us together to worship in church
continue in our daily lives,
so that we can be good neighbours
and good stewards of our neighbourhoods,
through the love of him who brings healing and wholeness,
your Son, Jesus Christ.
Amen

556 God of friendship and hope,
in our community
may we cherish new friendships and new neighbours,
as well as sustaining long-standing relationships.
Your apostles blazed a trail of bringing the good news.
May we, through hospitality and courtesy,
witness to the love that you have showed us

in sending us your Son,
who made all things new
and rescued our relationship with you,
God of mercy and restoration.
Amen

557 Almighty God,
who brings out the extraordinary in the ordinary,
we thank you for the joy
of greeting friends and neighbours;
of sharing meals in homes and halls;
of helping out and being helped;
of playing and listening to music together;
of honouring difference and celebrating diversity;
of joining together to worship you,
God of community – and all communities.
Amen

558 God of subsidiarity,
you have given us free will
to be set apart or in community,
to be independent or interdependent.
May we never seek to be anything but dependent on you
for our creation, preservation
and for guiding our relationships with each other
in our *(village/suburb/town/city)*.
And may there always be room in our hearts for you,
as there was not at the inn that turned away
the mother of your Son,
Jesus Christ.
Amen

Communities and networks

559 God of communion,
may we see you in others
so that we may love our neighbour.
May we believe you in others

so that we can learn your wisdom.
May we love you in others
so that we may learn your grace.
Amen

560 Loving and nurturing Lord,
set our sights high and our walls low
as we reach out to you through others.
May our network be your community too.
Let relationships thrive as we share our interests.
Let understanding grow
as different minds address an issue.
Give us the desire to work together
in a demanding common task.
Amen

561 God of connections,
may the power of human instincts
always be more powerful than the technology that serves us.
Bring us to a proper realisation
of the potential and the limitations
of a community of souls,
dedicated to each other, and to you.
May peace reign and love rule.
Amen

562 Lord of life,
bring us a true sign of your presence
through community and communion.
May we learn by reaching out,
build relationships with others through knowing you,
and create a better place
by the interchange of thought
and the benefit of debate.
May we truly worship
when we gather together,
in prayer and praise,
to hear your word and give thanks.
Amen

563 Father of all,
gather us together for mutual support,
but also for challenge and change.
May we be better prepared,
in this world and the next,
when we meet and greet,
share and care,
value our difference and diversity.
Never let the potential of technology
deprive us of human interaction,
the glue of community and the basis of humanity
in the world you have created,
saved by your Son,
Jesus Christ.
Amen

564 Lord of relationships,
thank you for reconnecting us to you through your Son.
Restore to us a true sense of place and purpose.
May our links with each other bring us a sense of community
by shared purpose, joint interest,
and a desire to explore all aspects of your world.
Let our networks be to your glory
and may we never forget
that these networks are only possible
because you gave us the free will
to live our lives in the light of your Son,
who always wants the best from us,
in the associations we have
and the relationships we make.
Amen

565 Heavenly Father,
help us to depend on each other,
in our lives, in our work, in our leisure interests.
And may the networks we form
never stray far from you,
who created the network of stars and light
that give us life and breath.

And may we build networks in our lives
which speak of you and witness to you
in how we communicate;
in how we show respect;
in how we love neighbour as self;
in how we respond to need.
Let us embrace the technology of change,
as your Son transformed our relationship with you,
Sovereign God.
Amen

566 God of gifts and generosity,
help us to rise to the challenge of change
in our communities as in our lives.
May our relationships be enhanced through new means of communication,
so that we can be in touch in new and exciting ways,
not limited to occasional meetings,
not limited by time and space,
enriching our communications for a purpose.
And may we seek new ways
of developing our relationship with you, Lord,
to enhance our worship in church,
to acknowledge your presence in all we do
and in every medium and network
you have given for our use,
immanent Lord.
Amen

567 Lord God,
be in our words
as we talk to each other.
Be in our hearts
as we care for one another.
Be in our eyes
as we seek to understand others.
Be in our imagination
as we catch a glimpse of your vision.
Be in our joy

as we see growth and development in family and friends.
Be in our compassion
as we share the suffering around us.
Be in our hope
as we hear your Son's promises.
Be in our networks of faith
as we try to be good disciples.
Be with us, without end.
Amen

Youth culture

568 Heavenly Father,
in bringing us life, you give us youth.
Pour your blessings on the next generation,
as they find their way in your world.
Let them make mistakes
but protect them from harm.
Let them challenge our assumptions
but learn from the past.
Let them use the public space
but not intimidate others.
We ask this through the one who is forever young,
Jesus Christ.
Amen

569 God who makes all things new,
may we be tolerant
of things we don't like in the young.
Help us to think of our youth,
when we were making our way in an adult world.
Help us to give encouragement
rather than find reasons to blame.
And where the music causes pain,
or behaviour falls short,
let us remember how the prodigal son
was welcomed home,
forgiving Father.
Amen

570 Exuberant, extravagant God,
bring creativity and a sense of wonder
to our young people,
in their lives and in their hearts.
May we all listen to the voice of youth,
uncut, unvarnished, as it is.
May the power of listening
model the power of talking,
so that we may all grow
in love, in truth, in relationship
with each other and, above all, with you, Lord.
Amen

571 God of truth and honesty,
may the insights of youth
be shared in our churches.
Let the love of learning
be matched by inspirational teaching,
at home, at school, and in church.
Let youth ride out
and wisdom march on
where you are in the lead.
Amen

572 Sensational Lord,
surround the youth of today
with the cloak of your love,
so that no matter if they stumble,
no matter if they offend,
they are being true to themselves,
true to each other,
and true to you.
May they strive for peace,
even if their efforts are noisy.
Help us not to ape their ways or interests
but be ready to learn from their insights.
Amen

Youth and uniformed groups

573 God of inspiration and aspiration,
we ask for your blessings on the youth of today
and on the people and organisations
who give them opportunities to grow.
Let the uniformed organisations flourish in our halls and churches
and let leaders come forward
to continue to develop the work
in every generation.
Help us to trust and let go,
as well as organise and oversee.
Above all, may there be fun and fellowship
alongside the challenges met, the badges won,
and the friendships made.
Amen

574 Father of all,
help all those involved with young people
to bring aspiration and understanding,
to equip for future achievement,
to promote responsibility and faith in the future,
and not to dwell on what might have been.
May uniformed organisations build up individual potential
as well as team endeavour.
May the Scouts and Venture Scouts, Guides and Rangers,
Cubs and Brownies, Rainbows and Beavers
all be blessed with committed leaders,
encouraging parents and firm friendships,
so that communities can be built up
and lasting relationships forged.
Amen

575 Heavenly Father,
may our churches be blessed with strong groups of young people, from toddler groups to youth groups,
from junior church to choirs and music groups.
May we always see them as part of *today's* church,

knowing that if we fail to do this
we ignore the future by dwelling on the past.
May we see the present as a gift to be cherished,
an opportunity not to be missed,
as we grow discipleship
in the young of today,
from whom we have so much to learn,
as your Son showed us.
Amen

576 God of community,
let young and old, children and adults,
play a full part in all aspects of our lives,
in our church communities, our homes and neighbourhoods,
our networks and prayers.
May we always be aware of differing needs and potential skills.
As your Son directed the disciples
to let children have access to him,
so may we seek to include rather than exclude
when we look to meet the needs of young people.
Above all, Lord, bring us the gift of discernment
as young people seek your purpose for them.
Amen

The marginalised

577 Lord of the unloved,
help us to be more like you,
to include where we would tend to exclude;
to recognise gifts instead of faults;
to seek out those on the edge of society;
and to bring wholeness to the broken in spirit.
Your Son has showed us the way,
in his reaching out and his bringing in.
Let us be open and welcoming,
even when we feel challenged and uncomfortable.
We ask you to strengthen our resolve

and equip us to be gracious and accepting
in all our doings in this world,
as you are to us, God of grace.
Amen

578 God of vision and understanding,
may we always seek to know you in the stranger;
may we listen to you in the bystander;
may we recognise you in the timid and tender.
Give us all the courage of a faith
which looks to your Son as a model,
to your Holy Spirit as the enabler,
and to you for our creation and preservation.
You have given us difference and diversity.
Let us seek to embrace and get to know the differences,
so that we can better understand the whole of your world
and the extent of your love for all,
through your Son, who shows us the way.
Amen

579 Almighty God,
you can shape our future as you have shaped our past. Bring
us wisdom to know our limitations
as well as the gifts of others.
May we see you in unlikely places and people.
May we learn from those who seem to have no stake in society.
Give us insight and discernment
as we try to encourage, enable and equip,
not only through skills and qualities we have been given,
but also through an awareness and humility
which we can sustain
only with the help of your Son, Jesus Christ.
Amen

580 Heavenly Father,
you have given us a big issue to work on,
showing us abundance of riches
alongside deprivation and poverty.
Put us in the shoes (if they have them)

of those our society shuns.
Put us in the minds
of the broken in health and spirit.
Put us in the hearts
of those who hurt and who are hurt by others.
Give us, we pray, the 'inside out' understanding
to turn the world upside down, as your Son did,
meeting you in our encounters with the downtrodden;
encountering our real selves
in our meetings with the marginalised.
Amen

The excluded

581 Lord of all,
you embrace all of humanity,
enfolding us in love and grace.
Teach us to open our hearts
to those at the margins of society,
because that is where you are,
and where we should be too.
We thank you for the many gifts and benefits of life,
but, in gratitude and thanksgiving,
we know we fall short of your generosity.
Your Son taught us the way of inclusiveness.
Help us to see the truth of his teaching
so that we can lead the life he wants us to lead,
through Jesus Christ.
Amen

582 God of mercy, God of grace,
keep us to the true path;
not one that constrains and ignores those by the wayside,
but the true path that keeps us alert
to all that happens along the way;
to those who are resting;
to those who are suffering;
to those who are hiding;

to those who are being kept from us – and from you.
Let us always seek ways to open hearts
and to open doors, for you to come to us,
and for us to go out,
whenever you call,
wherever that leads.
God of adventure, we thank you.
Amen

583 Heavenly Father,
you came down in your Son,
to include us in your kingdom.
May we respond by inviting all to join you:
the well-heeled and privileged
who may need to learn humility;
the poor and marginalised
who need to know you care;
and ourselves, with all our imperfections.
You can make all things new,
so we ask that you turn things upside down
and inside out,
as we answer your Son's call to welcome the stranger
and to learn from the outsider,
so that the excluded feel part of your kingdom
and special in your eyes.
Amen

584 Immanent Lord,
creator of the outer reaches of the universe
as well as the stars nearer home,
bring us to realise that you are in all humanity,
rich, poor, gay, straight, black, white;
and your Church is for all ages,
all backgrounds, all states of grace.
Give us the courage and the means
to welcome where once we turned away,
to love where once we hated,
to support where once we walked away.
Let your Holy Spirit work within us,
to help us appreciate all that is around us,
inclusive Lord.
Amen

The stranger

585 God of friendship,
your Son showed us the meaning of hospitality
towards disciples and strangers alike.
May we, like him, offer a hand of welcome
and a sign of friendship
when we meet strangers in our neighbourhood or church,
just as we would hope for the same
when we are strangers in other places.
But whatever our own experience,
let us be good hosts to strangers,
not because we expect to earn our own welcome
but because your Son has shown us, and you guide us,
to do always what is right in your sight.
Amen

586 Lord and Father of humankind,
you sent your Son as a stranger in a hostile world:
born in an outhouse,
shunned by ordinary people
and killed by the great and the good.
only the excluded, the outcast,
faithful fishermen and loyal womenfolk,
welcomed him and took him to their hearts
as the prophets would have wanted.
So let us learn our lessons and free our hearts
to be accepting of the stranger,
to be open to the different,
to be gracious to the alien,
to be generous to grateful and ungrateful alike.
Help us to be a bit more like your Son,
whose welcome is constant to those who turn to him.
Amen

587 Lord of light,
shine your beam of positive energy
on all of us in our dealings with strangers.
May we beware of those who mean us harm,

but let us trust our instincts and your direction
when we come across those who need your love.
May we discern their inner feelings
and seek to engage with people in a spirit of empathy.
Grow in us, Lord, a sense of trust,
a tendency to listen as well as hear,
and a willingness to be challenged,
as your Son was.
Amen

588 God of great expectations,
pour down on your people
a generosity of spirit which breaks down barriers.
Create in us the capacity
to grow in faith in you
and to have more faith in other people,
in particular those we don't know,
but whom we meet in different situations.
May we incline our hearts to them
rather than turn our backs on them.
Give us the trust in you
and the confidence in ourselves
to take risks in getting to know strangers
and to be ready to learn new things
from people we may neither know nor like.
Send us out in the Spirit that sent your Son into the world
and the Spirit that lives with us now.
Amen

The different

589 God of great generosity,
look at the sheer diversity of your creation
and help us to celebrate differences.
In our heart of hearts we know the importance of difference,
yet sometimes we ignore or shun the different.
May we embrace diversity,
cherish, encourage and challenge other ways,

and not be afraid of 'the other'.
Take away our distrust of what we are not used to
and make us open to the shock of the new,
as well as the legacy of the past,
even as we make the most of the present.
We ask this through the one
who both acknowledged difference and ignored it,
your Son, Jesus Christ.
Amen

590 Dear Lord,
make it our pleasure and responsibility
to bring an openness of spirit
to all our encounters with those we meet.
In our places of work,
in our houses and in our churches,
may we be available to others,
slow to judge,
and quick to respond to need.
May we offer the gift of hospitality,
as we have received it so many times ourselves,
from strangers and friends,
from family and neighbours,
from your Son, via his disciples,
and directly to us, generous God.
Amen

591 God of greatness and mercy,
your Son always saw the best in people
and forgave those who repented their worst.
Help us to respect those who are different from us,
acknowledging that we are all different and special in your eyes.
Give us the empathy and the interest
to communicate well with others,
making fresh connections and sharing our common humanity.
Develop our insights and strengthen our resolve
to love others as you love us.
Amen

592 Great Shepherd of the sheep,
may we be both pastor and friend
to those of a different ethnic origin,
to those of a different sexuality,
to those of a different age,
to those of a different faith,
to those of a different nationality.
As you are alongside the lonely and oppressed,
the minority as well as the majority,
help us to make room in our hearts
to get to know the different in your world,
because we all share in one bread,
the bread of life.
Amen

Minorities

593 God of the downtrodden,
you know through your Son
what it is to be the minority,
not only through his own persecution and suffering,
but through his rapport with the oppressed and outcast.
We ask that we are strengthened
in our sensitivity to those in a similar situation,
whether through background, status, position or sexual orientation.
Let majorities understand their special responsibility
not to impose their will
but to follow you,
generous and inclusive Lord.
Amen

594 Heavenly Father,
to you everyone is special – and all are different.
Help us, where we are in the majority,
to be generous and gracious to minorities.
Help us, where we are in the minority,
to appreciate the needs and aspirations of the many.

In both cases may we seek to make our contribution,
in the knowledge and assurance of your kingdom,
in the hope and faith of the disciples.
May our own discipleship
be strong enough to resist bullying and condemn oppression,
with your help.
Amen

595 Lord of all,
of small and large, strong and weak,
of great numbers and single figures,
may we respect minorities when we are in the majority
and respect majorities when we are part of a minority.
May we never forget that all of us change
from majority to minority and back according to our role.
Let us take our cue from your Son's championing of minorities,
from the Good Samaritan to the tax collector,
from the leper to the prostitute,
from children to the hungry.
Thank you for his example,
through whom we pray, Jesus Christ.
Amen

596 God of greatness,
you know that small is beautiful too.
As we appreciate the infinitesimal
alongside the universal,
and recognise the extraordinary in the ordinary,
so may we cherish any minority,
however strong or fragile,
gentle or vociferous,
and seek always to do your will
in the way we respond to their cries
and the way we understand their needs.
But just as warlike might is not always right,
so we should use judgement and fairness
in responding to demands from minorities,
showing the justice your Son did not receive
from the great and the good.
Amen

The prejudiced

597 Forgiving Lord,
help us in our prejudice.
May we constantly be aware
of all that causes us to dislike others.
Show us the way to love others,
even when we can't bring ourselves to like them.
Give us the insight to understand others;
give us the grace to respect others;
and even where we still feel envious or diminished
may we learn from the example of your Son,
who faced prejudice and hate,
resentment and betrayal,
to save us from our sins – including prejudice.
Amen

598 Lord of all,
extend your love to those consumed by hate.
Help them to look at the origins of prejudice
so that they can tackle whatever troubles them.
May they be able to turn from resentment
to the path of dialogue and discussion,
resisting the temptation to stoke up hatred.
May your will break through prejudice and pride
to bring healing and help where needed,
even if your love is resisted and rejected,
as your Son was, in order for our relationship with you
to be restored – for good.
Amen

599 Heavenly Father,
you know our innermost thoughts
and all our imperfections.
Create in us all a desire to reduce and eliminate prejudice:
prejudice against you;
prejudice against fellow humans;
prejudice against other countries;
prejudice against those who do things differently from us;

prejudice against the old or the young;
prejudice against those who seek the truth.
Empower and enable those who confront prejudice,
and those who seek to mediate and reconcile,
with patience, perseverance
and the power of the Holy Spirit,
to make a difference in your name.
Amen

600 God of great change,
pour the power of your transforming love
on those entrenched in prejudice and pride.
May they learn the lessons of history
where ignorance has bred suspicion,
leading to resentment and envy,
hatred and violence.
Give us all the capacity to work through our frustrations,
improve our sense of right and wrong,
and set an example of openness and acceptance
in our dealings with victims and oppressors alike,
while condemning the prejudice as it shows itself.
Give us the strength to make a stand,
with the help of Jesus Christ, your Son,
our Saviour.
Amen

SPECIAL OCCASIONS

Life changes

601 Eternal God,
you are Lord of change and changelessness.
Bring me insight and understanding
as the milestones of life are reached:
my own and of those around me.
Let me savour and appreciate each one,
knowing that you are with me all the way.
From the miracle of birth to the mystery of death,
each step is into new territory for me,
but not for you, whose Son broke the barriers of sin
and death for all time
and shares my joy and pain.
I ask this in Jesus' name.
Amen

602 Understanding Lord,
create in me the capacity to cope with change,
to realise the potential you have given me
at every stage of my life,
never thinking that I can do it all myself
or that everything will go smoothly.
But listening to others and to you along the way,
I know that some changes will be expected and planned,
while others will hit me suddenly and hard.
Let my preparation be in building the capacity to respond,
not in the acquisition of material things
for all eventualities.
Help me to heed warning signs,
as well as look for encouraging ones,
and may curiosity for what lies ahead
outweigh any fear of the unknown.
Through the one who changed us all,
your Son, Jesus Christ.
Amen

603 Heavenly Father,
who gave us night and day, sun and moon,
who brought us summer and winter, spring and autumn,
let us celebrate change and transformation –
the natural order of things.
Just as you created change,
so let us appreciate the continuity too.
We thank you, Lord, that your Church marks every change –
from christening to confirmation, from weddings to funerals –
while staying a symbol of your presence in the world,
an evolving witness to the ministry of your Son,
our Saviour, Jesus Christ.
Amen

604 Constant Lord,
forgive us our need for your attention,
especially when we are facing changes or encountering difficulty.
It's just that life changes often come in your time, not ours,
even when you surprise us,
because it reminds us that we are human and you are God,
though it can be inconvenient.
You and I know that progress is not as certain as change,
but please don't remind us of that too often.
Thank you, Lord.
Amen

605 Transforming God,
keep me open to your Holy Spirit,
so that I can do what you really want of me.
It would be so easy for me to shut up shop,
to refuse to budge from my ways
rather than seek your way.
So often I take the soft option,
when you want me to make the hard choice.
I need your support and direction, Lord,
so that when the big changes come

I can cope with the implications
for me and those around me.
Give me the capacity to change and be changed
through your Son, Jesus Christ.
Amen

Marriage

606 Lord God,
you created man and woman
to tend your world and each other.
Help us to be true to your vision
in the way we love,
in the way we take joint responsibility,
in the way we care for each other,
in the way we nurture children,
in the way we worship you,
and in the way we honour and cherish our own parents,
knowing that you remain Father of all,
including your Son, Jesus Christ.
Amen

607 Heavenly Father,
bless our friends . . . and . . .
as they take their vows before you.
May they come to love you more
as they grow in their love for each other.
Grace their union with the blessing of children
if it is your will,
and may their home be a source of comfort
and hospitality for family and friends.
In their life together, let each flourish –
and may they jointly prosper,
sharing the gift of marriage and the blessing
of companionship,
through the love of your Son, Jesus Christ.
Amen

608 Lord of life and love,
on the wedding day of . . . and . . . ,
shine your blessings on their lives
and warm their hearts in love.
May they draw on the best experiences of growing up
as they prepare for parenthood,
and may they know the love of each other's parents
as they create a home for themselves,
sharing hospitality and being good neighbours
as you would want them to be.
Amen

609 Lord,
help us to mend our breaking marriage.
Open our hearts to each other – and to you.
It has been tough for us both recently.
Let us reflect on what has gone wrong . . .
Put into our minds and hearts how we can make it work,
what I should do,
what we should do.
Please, Lord, let us try harder to remember our vows
made before you, and stick to them
out of a wish to do so, not out of fear of doing wrong.
Rekindle our love, redeeming Lord.
Amen

610 Gracious God,
we commend to you all who embark on married life,
knowing that it is your will that unions between men
and women should be blessed in your name.
As your Son was a wedding guest in Cana,
so may he be a frequent visitor
in marriages and families known to us,
welcomed in and honoured at times of celebration,
comforting and consoling in times of despair and loss,
caring and healing when sickness strikes,
and inspiring and nurturing in the knowledge and love
of you,
so that you are known as a friend of the family,
Father of all.
Amen

Birth

611 Father God, who makes all things new,
we ask for your blessing on this birth;
that this act of creation will transform our lives
and all that we are,
knowing we have new responsibilities,
alongside new joys and explorations.
May our baby be your child, too, Lord,
and may *he/she* come to know and love you.
Protect *him/her* as *he/she* makes *his/her* way in life,
and let our nurturing do justice
to the world that this new soul has entered.
Through the Son whose birth was a new beginning
for us all,
Jesus Christ.
Amen

612 Loving Lord,
the hour is come for new life to emerge
in the miracle that is a newborn child.
You watched as your Son was born in Bethlehem,
that first Christmas when the world changed.
May this baby be welcomed and cherished,
and brought up with the selfless love
that Mary and Joseph showed all those years ago.
Strengthen us to do our very best
to take our fair share of responsibility
while entrusting *him/her* to your special care
as *he/she* grows in faith, with the help of godparents
and the wider church family,
your family, Lord.
Amen

613 God of beauty,
thank you for the safe birth of . . . ,
for parents . . . and . . . ,
and for all the medical, nursing and midwifery staff
involved.

Let the celebration be joined in heaven
by all those who went before,
and whose memory means so much to us today.
Ring out bells of hope
and chimes of freedom
for the new generation.
Create in us the right response
to a baby's cry and a sweet smile
that spell out transformation.
We ask this in Jesus' name.
Amen

614 God of small wonders,
let it sink in that life has been created
in this delicate but resilient human being.
Help us to reflect that your Son
was just such a vulnerable baby,
who went on to change the world.
Anything is possible with you, Father God.
Amen

615 Almighty God,
help all those who struggle to give birth,
those who have tried and not been able to conceive,
those who have lost their baby naturally,
and those who have had a termination.
We bring to you also, Lord,
the mothers who, through poverty and starvation,
have been unable to sustain the life of infants,
and through disease and disorder
have seen the lives of offspring ebb away.
We thank you for the gift of life.
We know that everyone is precious in your sight,
whether their lives are short or long,
deprived or well provided for,
loving Lord.
Amen

616 Lord,
let the miracle of birth be a beacon of hope.
Bring to us an awareness of the potential of the new
in the transformation that is the creation of life.
Let us reflect on what birth can mean
to us,
to mothers,
to fathers,
to you.
And let us rejoice in the force for good
that family life can be
if you are at the heart of it.
Through the Son whose birth brought you joy,
Jesus Christ.
Amen

Birthdays

617 God of all ages,
pour your blessings on all those with birthdays this week:
thirty or ninety,
eight or eighty,
one or seventeen;
everyone is special in your eyes,
and may everyone with a birthday feel special too.
Give to all those around a reason to celebrate,
not just the day, but the person, not just the years,
but the gifting,
not just the milestone, but the journey,
not just the past, but the future.
May we gain perspective,
as we mark the years,
and count the blessings,
through your Son, our Saviour, Jesus Christ.
Amen

618 Lord of all time,
we thank you for the celebration of birthdays,
for the celebration of life itself,
and for the person(s) celebrating a birthday today.
May . . . enjoy the day,
cherish the memories,
and look forward to what the future holds.
Renew in all of us a spirit of thankfulness,
knowing that the present is a gift,
and an experience to be shared.
At the very time when people are focused on one person,
let it be a time for communal celebration,
and another reason to thank you,
generous God.
Amen

619 Heavenly Father,
as the angels rejoiced at the birth of your Son,
may every birthday bring joy,
every step along life's journey
bring new discoveries and new reasons to believe.
May your plan for us give us hope,
from day to day and year to year,
but also closer to our inner selves,
when your Holy Spirit can bring us alive,
if we care to turn to you.
Make every birthday a time for renewal,
a time to be born again,
through the love of your Son, Jesus Christ.
Amen

620 Dear God,
help us to celebrate this birthday as you would want,
in the lighting of candles
– and blowing them out in one go;
in the sharing of cake
– and handing it out to friends;
in the singing of silly songs
– and not being embarrassed;

and in the giving and receiving of presents
– and remembering to say 'thank you'.
Above all, let us have fun, Lord,
– and commit our next year to do great things,
and walk in your way,
our shepherd, priest and king.
Amen

Anniversaries

621 Lord of all time,
we give you thanks for this milestone.
May . . . and . . . look back with pride
and look forward with hope.
Let this day be a special day,
and may it be great for you too, Lord.
Help us to appreciate the commitment
two people have given to each other,
and may their relationship with you
be enfolded in love, inspire them in truth
and bring them at the last
to your eternal kingdom,
through Jesus Christ.
Amen

622 God of partnership and promise,
create in us a commitment to each other
in marriage,
in civil partnership,
in family,
in friendship,
at work,
in church,
as neighbours,
in teams.
And may we celebrate significant anniversaries in all these areas,
especially today, as we remember

the anniversary of . . . and . . . .
Give us open minds and generous hearts,
as we join in the celebration.
Amen

623 Gracious Lord,
you know and see things that really matter.
Today we ask for your blessing
on . . . and . . .
as they celebrate an important anniversary.
May their love be an example to others
and may their love for you
be stronger for their partnership.
Give to all your people
the capacity for self-giving love
through the example of your Son, Jesus Christ.
Amen

624 Father, Son and Holy Spirit,
you have offered to us
a perfect sign of indivisibility,
a perfect partnership made in heaven,
but clearly evident here on earth.
May we take your example
in our long-term commitments to each other,
to our family,
to our church,
to our workplace,
to our charity of choice.
May trust develop from understanding,
sacrifice be offered through love,
and service be given without hesitation.
Bring us to a true appreciation
of what binds us together,
as you are bound together in trinity.
Amen

Employment

625 Heavenly Father,
you asked your disciples to make huge changes
when you invited them to follow you.
What task do you have for me as
I think about the next step?
(*Silence*)
My qualifications are important as means,
but what are the ends you have in mind?
(Silence)
With my work life ahead of me,
I want to make the right choices
and give the right weight to each factor.
Please keep my mind open and my heart engaged,
but most of all, Lord, I want to heed your call.
I ask this in Jesus' name.
Amen

626 Lord of high endeavour,
help me in my efforts at work at this time
as I take on more and more responsibility,
and expectations rise about my ability to deliver.
You have given me gifts that have held me in good stead,
talents which I hope you feel I have developed and used.
Let me get the right balance between work and home,
so that loved ones feel loved
and work colleagues feel supported.
May the confidence you have given me
survive any test and challenge ahead,
through the inspiration of your Son, Jesus Christ.
Amen

627 God who gives and takes away,
you know what it is to suffer loss.
Let us pray for those who have lost their jobs recently,
especially . . .
Be close to those most affected, Lord:
the families,

the community,
the friends.
May neighbours watch over their welfare
and support services be sensitive to their needs,
so that new opportunities are offered and grasped
in the knowledge of the love of your Son, Jesus Christ.
Amen

628 Almighty God,
let us not forget the impact of our economy
on the employment of our brothers and sisters
in other countries.
Help us to buy fairly and trade fairly,
so that there is just reward for work done well,
and long-term hope for whole communities
rather than short-term gain for international companies.
We ask, Lord, that there is gradual transition
from inequality to equality in the world
and from unjust to just systems,
so that the gifts and labours of all
are properly rewarded and duly honoured.
We ask this through the one we honour and serve –
Jesus Christ.
Amen

629 God of great expectations,
may we aim high in all we do,
volunteer where we can make a difference,
bring on the talents of others we know,
and treat our colleagues fairly.
Especially, Lord, we pray for a sure touch
as we cope with change,
knowing that some people can handle this better
than others.
Give me the strength not to take the easy way
if the hard way is the correct course,
and let me never forget to acknowledge the efforts
of others
as partners in the process of change and development,

recognising the model of your Son,
who sent out the seventy-two
to do his work and spread your word.
Through the one who fulfilled your expectations,
and always exceeds ours,
Jesus Christ.
Amen

Retirement

630 Lord of rest and peace,
I am not used to this new way of life.
Help me to see the potential of it all.
You have been with me during my working years,
steered me through my career,
with all its ups and downs.
Be with me now in the choices I make,
in the way we relate at home,
and in the new tasks that await me.
Thank you for helping me to be useful in your world.
May I find time to work in your service, more and more,
through the one whose service is perfect freedom,
Jesus Christ.
Amen

631 Heavenly Father,
let me pause and reflect on this milestone of retirement.
To me it is strange and new,
especially after all the nice things people said
when I stepped down.
What awaits me now?
(Silence)
What do you wish me to do, Lord?
(Silence)
And the family?
(Silence)
Are there gifts that I have which could be of help
to your Church?

Please make known your call as I pray to discern your will for me.
(Silence)
I ask this in Jesus' name.
Amen

632 Redeeming and forgiving God,
as I retire from one episode of my life,
I realise that I was led and influenced by the world too much,
striving to do rather than be,
seeking to impress more than to support and inspire,
not letting you into my life –
except where things went wrong.
So forgive me for not thanking you enough,
and let me now know you better
through daily prayer and reflection
and through listening carefully to what others say,
both in the church and in the wider community,
not forgetting the family and neighbours I have neglected.
I ask this through your Son, who gave us a second chance,
Jesus Christ.
Amen

633 Almighty God,
we pray for all retired people at this time:
for the enterprises that will continue to flourish
because of their contribution;
for the work friends they left behind;
for the love and challenge you gave to them
and expected of them;
and, most of all, Lord, for their future work in your vineyard.
May they be open-minded and generous with their time and skills;
may they experience aspects of your world that are new to them;
and may they grow in the love and knowledge of you
on their journey home.
Through Jesus Christ, our Lord.
Amen

634 God of mystery,
let retirement be an opportunity for exploration,
not a winding down of curiosity.
May we be a continuing learning community,
whatever our age or stage in life.
But in celebrating the freedom of retirement,
let us be aware of those who are suddenly alone,
those who do not have the means to take advantage of their retirement,
those who find it difficult to adjust to life changes,
and those whose children do not seem to be interested in them.
How can we make retirement fun, Lord,
for us and for all those we have more time for?
Keep us up to the mark so that we can truly love others as we love ourselves.
We ask this knowing that you never rest, retire or give up on us, eternal Father.
Amen

FAITH AND DOUBT

635 Lord of inner strength,
you showed, through your Son, the power of faith.
Bring me to understand and feel that strength
in the way I face difficulty and disappointment,
and in the way I deal with the despair of others.
You have been gracious to me, Lord, in the good times,
when I probably did not thank you enough.
Let your light pierce my soul
and bring awareness of our relationship in its fullness,
forgiving God.
Amen

636 Heavenly Father,
with your help, let me examine the state of my faith today.
When do I turn to you?
Why do I turn to you?
When do I really worship you?
When do I share my faith?
What are the doubts I have?
Please, Lord, show me how I can deepen my faith –
and share it with others.
Through the love and example of your Son, Jesus Christ.
Amen

637 Mighty Counsellor,
turn me inside out and upside down,
if it means I can know you better.
As I look deeply into my soul,
I sometimes feel there is nothing there,
and no real desire to grow in faith.
Let me feel something of the fervour of the first disciples.
Open up the insights of the early Fathers
and create the hunger in me
to learn to love you more and more each day.
Through your Son, my tutor, Jesus Christ.
Amen

638 God the giver,
make us want to explore our faith journeys
in all our church activities and daily devotions.
We are often praying for people far away,
but do we realise they may be praying for us?
We pray for the poor and suffering in the world,
but please direct us in how we should respond
in other ways.
Bring to us a realisation that the poor and the suffering
may be praying about our indifference, our poverty
of spirit, our turning away from you.
Create in us an understanding of the gifts and gaps
in our lives
and how we can draw on your guidance to get a better
balance.
Amen

639 Amazing Lord,
as I seek to explore your ways,
may I do so with true humility,
rather than assuming that all I have to do is listen.
I realise I must work at my faith
and put in the hard yards, alongside the flashes of insight.
Point me to the books of those who have struggled with
these issues,
even those I find difficult at times,
like Paul and . . .
Make me read or listen to someone I don't really
understand or agree with,
but who may have a lot to teach me.
Help me to be open to new ideas
and push me up that steep learning curve to a better
understanding of you, immanent God.
Amen

640 God of revelation,
in all the trials and tribulations I have experienced recently,
the only thing that has kept me going is faith in you.
Strengthen my resolve to keep the faith,
even when it seems that all is lost.

Give me a sense of your Son's purpose,
as he carried out your mission to bring us back to you.
In all my difficulties, keep me focused on his resolve
to do your will.
Let me learn my lesson and take my cue
from his great task,
and play my humble part in your grand design,
with the help of your Son, Jesus Christ.
Amen

641 Merciful Lord,
look favourably on . . .
as troubles mount and *his/her* faith is tested.
You inspired that faith in *him/her* who needs your
comfort now.
I pray that *he/she* turns to you and seeks your help.
May *he/she* find that assistance through family
and friends and through the family network.
Most of all, may *he/she* feel your presence
at *his/her* side,
in *his/her* heart,
in *his/her* prayers,
in *his/her* sleeping,
in *his/her* waking,
and in the church where *he/she* feels at home.
Through your Son who has never ceased to love,
Jesus Christ.
Amen

642 Rock of our lives,
you are the cornerstone of our faith
and the mainstay of our hearts.
Help us to grow in our desire to know you better.
Make us search and search again
to understand the full extent of your love for us,
so that when we face the changes and chances of life
we are able to turn to you with confidence of consolation.
As we pray for your hopes to be fulfilled,
may we seek to meet the challenges you set us,
through the help of your Son, Jesus Christ.
Amen

643 Heavenly Father,
give us a glimpse of heaven
in the smile of others and the faith of saints.
Give us a sound of eternity
in the stillness of waters and the beauty of music.
Give us a sign of transcendence
in the soaring of a spire and the starkness of the cross.
Give us hope for the future
in the cry of a baby and a school bell sounding.
Give us a clue to the right way
in a prayer answered and a Bible passage understood.
Give us a true appreciation of your generosity
in giving us your Son, our Saviour, Jesus Christ.
Amen

644 Lord of beginnings and endings,
you brought us hope at the first.
Bring us faith at the last.
You created in us a desire to know and love you.
Bring us a desire to worship you in word and song.
Let every new step bring a fresh experience.
Let every new convert bring joy to us all.
Let every new day be greeted with thanks.
And while evenings are to be savoured,
our night-times full of peace and rest,
so we pray that there is always a new dawn,
whether in this world or the next.
We ask this through the one who brought us the fruits
of a new heaven and earth,
your Son, Jesus Christ.
Amen

645 Forgiving Lord,
help me in this time of doubt:
doubt in myself; doubt in you;
doubt in every aspect of life just now.
It may seem strange that I still turn to you
when part of me feels that no one is listening.
If you are there, break through that veil of doubt

and show that all is not lost,
that you are there to support me,
you are there to inspire me,
and somewhere in me is the will to believe in you.
I doubt, therefore I am human,
but to believe would be very heaven.
Amen

646 God of great faith,
look down on those of us who doubt
and help us to look up and see you.
We desperately want and need you,
but mostly pretend we can go it alone.
In times of trouble and torment
we are the first to ask you to sort things out,
just in case you can make a difference.
Then when everything is fine,
we tend not to thank you at all.
Give me some insight into the mind of our creator,
through Jesus Christ, our Lord.
Amen

647 Long-suffering Lord of all,
help me to face my doubt and understand
what form it takes as I reflect
on what I do believe in, what I don't believe in,
how I came to have doubt,
how I would be convinced that there is more to faith
than I imagine . . .
and how I might take steps
to 'know thee more clearly,
love thee more dearly'. *
Enlighten me and free me from doubt,
with the help of Christ.
Amen

*(*Richard of Chichester, 1197–1253)*

648 God of comfort,
you bring hope and health to the sick,
and even life to those near death.
Please console us in our doubts and difficulties
where faith is tested by worldly events
and when our Church is riven with disputes
and disagreement.
Help me to hold on to the essence of faith,
rather than slide into doubt and despair
when the world is in a mess and your Church seems
helpless to hope.
Bring me back to what Jesus would say and do,
and what he would call me to undertake for him
and for you.
Then I might get back on the right track,
but only with the help of your Son, Jesus Christ.
Amen

649 All-seeing God,
you know my thoughts,
you know my doubts,
you know me.
Let me dare to reflect
on your thoughts about the world . . .
on your doubts about mankind . . .
on your doubts about me . . .
Then tell me your hopes and dreams
for the future of your Church in the world . . .
for the future of our planet . . .
for my future and the future of my family . . .
Thank you for helping me to face my doubts
and for sharing your hopes and plans,
which your Son died to show us.
Amen

MEDITATIONS

At break of day

650 Lord of our lives,
help me to discern all that you are to me,
to glimpse the love that you have shown,
to understand your will in all that I do.
(Silence)
Lift my sights, Lord, when I worry about little things,
and let me learn to love those challenges you send.
Let me know your comfort in those things that trouble me.
Tell me how I can bring comfort to others.
(Silence)
I dedicate this day to you, listening Lord.
Amen

In a break at work

651 God of faith and wonder,
be with me as I seek to make a difference in all that I do.
Help me to honour your name
in my dealings with other people and the way I behave.
Show me when and how to share my faith.
Let me meditate on the challenging parables
through which your Son taught us:
the mustard seed;
the buried treasure;
the pearl of great price;
the sower and the seed;
the young lawyer;
the prodigal son.
Now I'm ready to resume my other tasks of this day.
Thank you.
Amen

In the garden

652 God of nature and nurture,
as I stop and look at the plants and trees,
the flowers and fruit,
let me admire your work.
(Silence)
Thank you for giving me the chance to work in your garden,
to share your creation,
to help build your kingdom.
Let me learn the lessons of tending this garden
for the rest of my life.
This is so obviously a partnership between you and me, Lord.
How can I fail to see that everything in life
is just the same, a shared effort,
as long as I realise that I am the junior partner,
your labourer in the vineyard?
Amen

On holiday

653 God of great adventures,
as you bring me new experiences on this holiday,
let me reflect on
the scenery you have created,
the people you have made in your own image,
the cultures that distinguish as well as divide us
and the values that we share.
Let this holiday be our day of rest, knowing that you rested too, Lord,
and let us rejoice in it.
Amen

At bedtime

654 God of rest,
how did you and I do today?
Tell me what went well from your perspective.
(Silence)
Let me share what I did wrong.
(Silence)
What do I need to reflect on tonight?
(Silence)
Tell me what you expect of me tomorrow.
(Silence)
Thank you, Lord. That's a weight off my mind.
Can I sleep now?
Amen.

For teachers and learners

655 Our Lord and our God,
you have created us in your image;
you have given us the freedom to know or deny you;
you see into our hearts and minds.
Set us on the right course to your still centre;
guard us and guide us when we do your will;
forgive us when we fall short of your plan for us.
Above all, God, hold us close, take away our fear.
(Silence)
Our God and Father,
teach us your ways, O God, so that we can know you better
and make you better known;
teach us to search for you in those around us,
in our families, in our churches, in our places of learning,
in unexpected places and people.
Teach us to love and trust you,
as we are loved and trusted by you, Lord;
teach us to take on new challenges, sacrificial
responsibilities, and fresh expressions of faith
for each new generation.

Above all, Lord, teach us to learn, encourage us to sow good seeds, empower us to witness to your love and forgiveness.
(Silence)
Our Father and Lord,
bring wisdom and enthusiasm to our schools, colleges and universities and to all who teach, learn and plan; bring a pastoral sensitivity and inspirational vision to our leaders, ordained and lay, elected and appointed, national and local.
May your Church make a difference in proclaiming that every child matters to you.
May talk of transformation focus on people's lives and be based on values taught by your Son.
In all of this; Lord, help us to take care and take risks to bring your kingdom closer to us and all those we serve.
(Silence)
The grace of our Lord Jesus Christ,
and the love of God,
and the fellowship of the Holy Spirit
be with us all evermore.
Amen

TRAVEL

Travelling and pilgrimage

656 Lord of all journeys,
be with me as I travel,
as your world is revealed to me,
as your diversity is impressed upon me,
as I see your presence all around me.
Help me to be open and receptive,
appreciative and trusting.
Trust me to be helpful to those around me.
Make me wary of those who may do me harm,
but grateful to those who wish me well.
What a world you have made!
Thank you for showing me and sharing a part of it.
Through your Son who made the ultimate journey,
our Lord, Jesus Christ.
Amen

657 God of great destinations,
we are a pilgrim people.
Give us a goal to achieve, a place to aim for,
but bring to us a real appreciation of the journey
along your way,
wherever that takes us, whoever we meet.
Let us relish every moment as we accompany you,
every person we encounter in your name,
each mountain and river, village and city.
Help us to spread our wings, look as far and wide
as we can,
and bring us safely home.
We ask this in Jesus' name.
Amen

658 Heavenly Father,
who leads us and follows us,
watch over our journey and our fellow travellers
as we set off with excitement and expectation.
You have been with us in our planning and in our
preparation.

May we be always grateful that you will be with us
in our journeying.
Help us to recall all we have read and all we have learned,
so that we can do full justice to the places we go
and bring back memories of experiences we can draw on
when we come home.
We ask this through your Son, our guide, Jesus Christ.
Amen

659 God of going out,
we pray for those who are travelling soon,
especially . . . as they go to . . .
Keep them from harm,
but put in their way all that interests and surprises
about your world,
so that they can learn from those who give them hospitality.
May their trip be a pilgrimage of hope and enjoyment,
a journey of fun and fascination,
and may they share their experiences with us
when they return,
as your Son will.
Amen

660 Lord without limits,
thank you for helping us to explore the boundaries
of your creation
through reading, listening, looking and learning,
as well as through travelling;
for preparing us before we journeyed;
for being present as we went;
and for being with us in our homecoming.
Spend time with us now as we reflect in silence
on all we have learnt . . .
from the places we went . . .
from the people we met . . .
from the things we did . . .
and from your presence with us now.
We give thanks for the boundless love you have shown
through your Son, Jesus Christ.
Amen

Exploration and endurance

661 Lord,
you took the biggest risk of all
by sending your Son to bring us back to you.
Help me to take risks as I explore your world,
knowing that you are there to watch over me.
Give me energy and inspiration
as I attempt things I never thought I would do,
as I challenge myself and those around me.
Let me trust and be trusted,
as there is only so much I can do alone.
And may I always trust in you,
ever-present and ever-ready God.
Amen

662 God of change and continuity,
make me push back the boundaries of my experience
and extend the limits of my horizons.
No place is strange to you, creator of all,
so why should anything in the world be strange to me?
Thank you for the many ways I can explore this richness
and the means to record and recall all that happens
as I do so.
But let me savour the moment of discovery of new things,
rather than add them to my list of things achieved;
and especially, Lord, help me to make new friends
wherever I go.
I ask this through Jesus Christ.
Amen

663 Reassuring Lord,
give me strength to be tough when I need to be.
As I enter new territory in every sense,
let me remember the way you provided for your people
in the desert.
You have always been faithful to pilgrims down the ages,
giving purpose and vision to travellers in their coming
and going.

As I set out on my journey to . . . ,
open my eyes to new people and places,
to new sights and sounds,
and to creatures I have never encountered.
Keep me safe, keep me healthy,
and keep me searching for your kingdom,
loving Lord.
Amen

664 God of letting go,
let's make this risk assessment together
as we pray for what's ahead:
the risk of staying in our safety zone . . .
the risk of not asking questions . . .
the risk of worrying too much . . .
the risk of forgetting your presence . . .
the risk of looking back or forward and not enjoying the moment.
Thank you, Lord, for helping us to sort out what is important
as we seek to live life in all its abundance.
Through your Son, Jesus Christ.
Amen

665 Liberating Lord,
we pray, as your Son taught us, for our daily bread.
Make it essential in all our exploration of your world
that we do everything in our power – and yours,
to bring this about, not just for ourselves,
not just for today,
but for everyone and for all time.
Bring growing awareness, capacity and commitment, as we journey,
to make a difference and a Christian statement that your will needs to be done,
in this world and the next.
And that it is only through sharing the bread of life
that we are one body, uniting God.
Amen

666 Long-suffering Lord,
teach me the art of endurance:
how the hard road is often the right route.
I am often tempted to take short cuts,
even when I know in my heart that I shouldn't.
Give me the stamina for the long haul,
the vision for the long term,
and the energy to sustain both.
Knowing that you are always there for me,
I put my trust in you.
Amen

667 Almighty God,
you made us in your image,
but we often let you down.
Give us the perseverance and the commitment to carry on,
even when everything seems to be against us.
Your Son taught us to pray to you
and suffered for us, even to death.
Help us, Lord, to live up to his example;
to be a living sacrifice in all we do,
to continue in his way against all obstacles,
to go the long way round if the alternative is to be without you.
Through the one who endured everything for us,
Jesus Christ.
Amen

668 Heavenly Father,
our endurance is tested every day
in our duty to you, as we watch and pray.
But we crave the perfect freedom that lies in serving you.
Put our faith journey first in our lives,
so that it can take us where you want,
so that our personal and family life can be underpinned in faith.
You are there for the long haul,
and we need to reflect that day by day –
by carrying through your tasks,

by advancing your kingdom, at home and abroad,
by understanding the interdependence of your creation,
and by standing firm in the name of Jesus Christ,
our Lord.
Amen

669 Lord of new things,
make us persistent and prepared,
as well as excited and spontaneous,
in our exploration of your world.
Give us endurance alongside the desire to experience
new places,
so that we may appreciate and understand
all that has gone before.
We know we are fortunate to benefit from our forebears,
so let us leave a lasting legacy
by doing justice to their achievements,
showing respect in our interpretation,
and building patiently on all their work – and yours, Lord.
Amen

670 Lasting Lord,
let me reflect on the endurance of your Son . . .
in his healing . . .
in his teaching . . .
in his response to accusation . . .
in the face of betrayal . . .
in his suffering on the cross . . .
in carrying out his Father's will.
Help to build up my endurance to complete your tasks
for me in my faith journey, especially at this time.
Remembering always your Son's endurance
for my sake.
Amen

671 Heavenly Father,
this is the first time I have travelled by air.
Thank you for the opportunity to survey your creation
from above.
Take away my fear of flying,

especially the taking off and landing.
You have given us the ability and means to fly,
to help us explore all the elements in your world.
I pray that the confidence and training of the crew
may make this a memorable experience
and a sign of your high expectations for us all,
made in your image and saved by your Son, Jesus Christ.
Amen

672 Lord of the air,
as we take off and rise up,
let my spirits leap too
at the opportunities ahead.
It is always your wish that we live life to the full,
and we wonder at all that you have provided,
both the means by which we can stretch our horizons
and the sheer range and variety of your creation
that we see.
Let us be safe and secure in the knowledge that,
even up here,
you guide us and journey with us, our true navigator.
Amen

673 Lord of all continents,
as we explore areas new to us,
we turn to you, for whom nothing is new.
Help us to adapt and be open,
to be receptive and aware,
so that the experience will be one from which we
can learn and grow.
I look forward especially, Lord, to . . .
And while I am abroad, please watch over those I leave
behind, especially . . .
Knowing that life goes on wherever you are present,
we ask this through your Son, Jesus Christ.
Amen

674 Heavenly Father,
lord of sea and sky, land and lake,
create in me a searching soul,
a desire to find out what lies above and beneath sea level.
Thank you for the gift of travel,
by road, rail, air, sea or ski.
Let me never be restricted by fear in exploring
your world,
but let me also be properly prepared,
practically and spiritually,
for the journeys that I make,
including the last one home, to you,
God of going out and coming in.
Amen

675 Almighty God,
who made the oceans greater than the land,
who held the seas back for Moses,
who provided fish to feed mankind,
let our voyage be one where the seas are kind to us,
and the winds are right for our trip.
Let us be aware of what lies beneath the waves,
and how storms can suddenly develop on the surface.
Keep this ship safe on its course,
and may it open up the world
to our exploration and your beneficence.
Amen

DIFFICULT TIMES

Dealing with difficult people

676 Inclusive Lord,
help us deal with difficult people;
not just those we don't like,
but those who really annoy us.
May we look into our hearts – and theirs,
to understand why they are difficult
and why we find it hard to relate to them.
Give us the patience and the ability
to set a good example,
in faith and trust.
Amen

677 God of variety and diversity,
may we always see the good in people,
but beware of the bad,
not in a judgemental way,
but in a developmental one.
Give us the means and the perseverance
to make a stand,
in a gentle way,
to encourage a change,
in an incremental way.
Amen

678 God of relationship,
send us a lifeline of harmony,
when relations are strained
and tempers flair.
Give to others and ourselves
a reason to reflect
and time to pause,
so that misunderstandings can be addressed,
differences disentangled from upset,
and peace restored.
Amen

679 God of stillness,
let silence break out when disputes flair up,
and when we encounter difficulty in others,
let us take deep breaths
before responding in kind;
and then may we show we are listening,
even when we don't quite believe what we hear.
Secure in us, we pray, a readiness to cope,
a desire to reconcile, as your Son did.
Amen

680 Lord of all saints and all souls,
help us to understand the present
through the lessons of the past.
We know now when difficult people
were not challenged or calmed,
when personal vendettas become national disputes,
often leading to wars and destruction.
Help us to avoid escalation of difference,
without compromising confrontation of evil.
Amen

Family breakdown

681 God of family and friendship,
may all that occurs in families
be blessed with an openness of spirit
and a wave of unconditional love.
Let us be open to challenges,
but always enfolded in the love which binds us,
and the love you have shown to us,
through your Son, Jesus Christ.
Amen

682 Astonishing Lord,
who made heaven and earth,
and brought man and woman into the world,
to your delight and our eternal gratitude,

let us be worthy of your trust
and the second chance you have given us,
to give firm foundations to family members
and true friendship to neighbours,
as your Son taught us.
Amen

683 Long-suffering Lord,
bring us patience and perseverance
in maintaining family relationships,
turning disunity into harmony,
jealousy or envy into trust.
May we set an example to the next generation
by promoting your values
and worshipping your holy name,
through Jesus Christ.
Amen

684 Amazing God,
you sent your Son as a member of the human family,
to have and to hold,
to worship and adore.
Let us model your generosity
in all our family dealings,
as the father of the prodigal son showed us
and the mother of your Son proved to us.
Amen

685 Lord of relationship,
make families secure;
may each generation be grateful to the last;
may family feuds turn into family friendships;
may our hearts be gladdened at family achievements,
but, above all:
let us know your blessings,
in our homes, in our households,
and in our family celebrations,
Father God.
Amen

Divorce

686 Lord of unity and diversity,
what you have brought together
may sometimes be put asunder,
given our fallen state.
We ask your forgiveness and patience,
long-suffering Lord.
We ask for the second chance
that you gave to humankind,
through your Son.
Amen

687 God of justice and mercy,
look down on the imperfection of humankind,
breathe a sigh, shed a tear,
and help us to face up to divorce,
if that is the only way forward.
May repentance and forgiveness
be the right way to part
and the only way to move on.
Amen

688 Lord God,
you brought man and woman together to care for each other
and to bring forth children, if that is your will.
Let delight in companionship
and the responsibility of parenthood
bring joy, not strife.
But if it proves to be not of you
that these two people should remain together,
may the parting of the ways
be as clear as the parting of the waves,
and may both parties pass through unscathed.
Amen

689 God of peace and reconciliation,
even if divorce is inevitable,
let there be peace in the process

and reconciliation of difference and diversity,
as separation and the parting of the ways
bring such sweet sorrow
and resignation to being apart.
Sorry, Lord, for what we have done
and for what we have left undone.
Amen

690 Lord of love,
we have let you down
when a marriage crumbles.
Help us to shoulder blame and responsibility,
if we have contributed
to the pressure and pain of separation.
But let us also take the responsibility
of mending lives,
through prayer, through listening,
through being there for people,
in the hope of reconciliation,
in the expectation of a second chance.
Amen

Abuse

691 Sovereign Lord,
we know that love turned bad
can lead to horrible things.
Let our hearts go out to those who have been abused,
and our powers of forgiveness be tested by those who have abused.
We all fall short in our lives.
But let us always call on you,
when feelings of hate or revenge threaten to take over.
Save us from ourselves and bring us back to your true path.
Amen

692 Astounding, transforming God,
where you have given us free will
we may stray from the right course.
May we be ever vigilant,
in ourselves and in our dealings with others,
so that evil does not take hold,
damage is not done,
and abuse is confronted.
We pray for victims and perpetrators,
that time and treatment will heal,
with your help, Lord.
Amen

693 Maker of heaven and earth,
you have shown us good and warned us of evil.
May we learn the lessons of the past,
in ourselves and over time.
Let us be aware of the signs of abuse,
unafraid of challenging behaviour,
but always seeking remedies
for body and soul, heart and mind,
knowing the extent of your reach.
Amen

694 God of transformation,
help those traumatised by abuse
be shown the power of true love,
by neighbour, friend and family,
so that the effects of abuse
can never close the channels to that love,
whatever went before.
Amen

695 Loving Lord,
against all odds may untainted, unconditional love prevail,
the love your Son showed us,
the love which restores,
the love which forgives,
the love which respects,
the love which can overcome abuse,
as long as we can trust you
and begin to trust each other again.
Amen

HEALING AND WHOLENESS

696 Almighty God,
who gives to each of us certain gifts and strengths,
help us to make the most of all that we are,
so that we can be the person you want us to be.
Let us learn lessons and seek inspiration
from those who, despite age and disability,
remain cheerful and faithful in all that they do.
Let them be an example to us
and a witness to your presence in our lives.
Be with us, Lord, in the dark times,
but let us also acknowledge your love in the good times.
And finally, Lord, may it be as good to arrive
as to travel in hope.
We ask this in the assurance of salvation,
through Jesus Christ, our Lord.
Amen

697 Healing, loving Lord,
be with those who are suffering
through sickness, distress or depression.
Calm and comfort them
and give the peace only you can provide.
May those who care for and minister to them
be given strength and patience.
May the medical and nursing professions
be graced with a concern for the whole person,
just as your Son always was
when healing the sick and forgiving sins.
May hope bring healing
and healing bring wholeness.
Amen

698 Lord of all,
we know you neither bring suffering
nor ignore the pain and distress of illness.
But we give thanks and pray for
your continued, comforting presence
alongside the sick and the injured.
Awaken in those who are unwell,

and in those who care for others,
a love for fellow humans
to match your own.
Your Son has always been our model and guide.
Let us be inspired by the miracles of his healing
as well as the tears he shed
for the sick and bereaved.
We ask this through the one who suffered for us,
your Son, Jesus Christ.
Amen

699 Caring Lord,
we pray for those in our church community
who are in urgent need of our prayers at this time.
For the sick: bring them healing;
for the injured: bring them swift recovery;
for the depressed: bring them hope;
for the bereaved: bring them comfort.
We ask that in the depths of suffering
they find the well-spring of your grace,
and that in the process of recovery
they find the warmth of caring love,
from family, friends, neighbours,
and above all from you,
God of consolation.
Amen

700 God of comfort,
bring to us all, in sickness and in health,
an appreciation of the needs of those who suffer and those who care.
May we be the first to help and the last to leave
when we are faced with the needs of others.
And may we be the first to ask for help
when we ourselves are in urgent need.
As givers and receivers,
may we always offer thanks to you
and ask for the inspiration and resilience
to help in the healing process,

to recognise the skills of others,
to be grateful for our own gifts,
and to respond without hesitation
to the call of the Holy Spirit
in testing situations of life and death.
Amen

701 Healing Lord,
lay your hands on me as I fight this illness.
Calm me and let the treatment take its course.
Help me to trust those who minister to me,
and be with them, Lord, in all that they do.
May those affected by my illness –
at home, at work, at church –
be reassured that you are present in my healing,
and let restoration to full health
be my aim and your will,
through your Holy Spirit.
Amen

702 God of power and might,
let the harm and hurt inside me be cast out,
so that I can once again hold my head up high.
Bring back the positive me
that always ran the course,
that never held back,
that saw the potential of anything
rather than the drawbacks of everything.
At the same time, I know that time can be a healer,
and that I cannot expect too much too quickly.
So, loving Lord, bring me patience to trust your timescale
and faith that I will get well.
Through your Son, the healer.
Amen

703 Heavenly Father,
help me to bear the pain of this illness,
which the experts say is chronic.
You and I have come through a lot together,
so let us tackle this in the same way.
I'll tell you how it feels today . . .
(Silence)
Now let me know how you can help,
Silence
and what you need me to do.
(Silence)
I am aware of so many prayers being said for me.
Help me to feel the power of that prayer.
Thank you, Lord.
Amen

The healthy and the sick

704 God of health and wholeness,
we ask for your blessings
on all who are hurting at this time,
through physical pain or mental distress.
May their spirits be raised
by what we do and say.
Most of all, Lord, hold out your healing hand,
and give them the promise
of your comforting presence.
Amen

705 Lord of restoration and recovery,
let us rejoice in physical and mental health,
the joy of being well,
the blessing of staying healthy.
But let us not forget the struggle of illness,
when food, drink and material things mean little.
May we build up our spiritual resources
so that when illness strikes
we can respond positively to others as to ourselves.
Amen

706 Serene Lord,
may we draw on the serenity of your presence
when we experience the confusion of our illness.
May we take heart from the miracles performed by your Son,
and continued through the disciples.
And may the modern-day miracles of treatment and care
go hand in hand with the privilege
of looking after one another,
in his steps and to your glory.
Amen

707 Suffering servant, healing Lord,
let us give thanks that where there is illness,
there is often a cure, courtesy of your creation;
and that when a cure is not available,
you give us other strengths and skills
to show our love for each other,
as well as the desire to search, search,
and search again,
for the strands and signs
in your world and in our minds,
which will unlock the answer.
Amen

708 Immanent God,
may your presence
teach us patience,
bring us transformation,
point us to the right treatment.
Help our bodies to help themselves;
keep us positive, even in suffering;
and may we always acknowledge
your presence in our ministry to others.
Amen

Mental health

709 Compassionate Lord,
bring us an understanding of your mind,
a glimpse of your truth,
which will help us to know
the extent of your love.
Embrace, we pray, the needs of those
who do not see clearly,
who find it difficult to relate to others,
and who go through phases of illness
in mind, in spirit, in relationship.
Bring calm and healing to troubled minds.
Amen

710 Suffering servant,
make all things new for us,
and especially for those with mental illness.
Make us compassionate through our engagement
and sensitive to the vulnerabilities
of those who are sick.
May we always see the person
behind the behaviour,
just as we see you
behind your creation,
knowing what is of you
and what is our contribution,
our value added or taken away.
Amen

711 Lord of health and wholeness,
look down, we pray,
on those who struggle with life.
Set them free from despair
through the glimpse of the hope you bring.
However it seems through the mist of hurt,
let your love dispel the cloud of unknowing
and restore a right relationship
with self, with you, with all around.
Amen

712 God of great expectations,
lift the spirits of all who suffer
from mental strife,
from guilt and pain,
from hate and insecurity.
Open the curtains to our soul
and let the light shine in.
Dispel doubt and fear
from the hearts of those who find it difficult
to face the next day
with the confidence you can inspire.
Amen

713 All-embracing God,
you understand the turmoil of those
whose mental state is a worry to others.
Release the energy of hope
in those who see only danger.
Bring self-knowledge and sensitive care
to the fragile and vulnerable in mind and spirit.
Above all, Lord, create in all of us, we pray,
the capacity to care, the patience to persevere,
as your Son did – and still does.
Amen

Dementia

714 Ever-faithful Lord,
forgive our forgetfulness, whenever and wherever it occurs.
And in our old age help us to focus on you,
even when other things are unclear to us.
May the residual memories and knowledge of you
break out of the cloud of unknowing
and set us free.
Amen

715 Eternal Father,
your Son taught us the importance of things that last
and the transience of the material world.
In the dementia that afflicts those of all ages,
but especially the elderly,
give hope and flashes of clarity
amidst the fog of forgetfulness.
Let the spirit of your presence
be evident in the hearts of those affected,
even if it is hidden from our sight.
Amen

716 Great and glorious God,
let the translucence of your presence
always show through the hesitations and repetitions of dementia.
May our patience and perception
not be found wanting,
as we seek the person within,
and the spirit of faith,
in gesture and twinkle, in touch and gaze,
guided by your bright star.
Amen

717 God of spirit and truth,
may the practice of the Eucharist
break through barriers of memory,
as we give thanks through bread and wine.
Let those with all their frailties intact
be especially sensitive to those whose gifts are restricted.
May we always respect the person,
as your Son respected all.
Amen

718 Lord of life,
renew in us a right spirit,
towards stranger and sufferer,
as well as neighbour and friend.
We never know when illness will strike,

gradually or all at once.
Let us look out for the needs
and struggles of those with dementia,
not through enlightened self-interest,
but through love of humankind,
love of your creation.
Amen

Alcohol addiction

719 Almighty God,
you have given us the bread of life,
but also our daily bread.
You have given us living water,
as well as water to drink.
But let us beware the effects of alcohol,
especially when we drink too much too often.
If we are addicted, help us to admit it;
if we seek to recover, make us strong in saying no.
Bless and preserve our will to be free
of harm to self or others.
Amen

720 All-embracing Lord,
forgive us our frailties and temptations
as we seek to shed our addictions.
Let the demon drink be overcome
as Satan was resisted in the desert.
But we must remember Satan's
'what though the field be lost, all is not lost'
in keeping up the battle against drink, drugs,
and all that enslaves.
Amen

721 All-enveloping Lord,
surround us with hope and trust
in your steely support
as we battle to resist addiction,
in ourselves and in loved ones.

May we be swift to learn
and slow to judge.
Let us be single-minded in our faith
and purposeful in our recovery,
seeking forgiveness for weakness
and showing discipline in rehabilitation.
Amen

722 God of remedy and reconciliation,
help the families of those addicted to drink,
in their sensitive situation.
Give them the patience of Job;
give to addicts Peter's ability to learn from failure;
give to friends a constancy that will be tested,
and let the tentacles of drink
release their grip on lives that
once were lost and now are found again.
Amen

723 God of fruit and vine,
as we sip our cocktail or swig our beer,
let us pause for thought.
As we quaff our wine
or savour our favourite spirit,
let us reflect.
All things should be in moderation,
except our love for you.
Amen

Cancer

724 Healing Lord,
let nature and the skills of doctors
join forces to mend and tend
all afflicted with cancer.
Let diagnosis be quick and treatment timely,
and may the knowledge of your presence
be a comfort and a shield,
to patient and carer alike.
Amen

725 God of the personal,
help us never to make assumptions about people's illness
or the treatment they receive.
May every step of recovery from cancer
be blessed with understanding and thanks,
and every setback be accompanied
by renewed prayer and encouragement.
May we combine the cure of disease with the cure of souls.
Amen

726 God of great gifts,
send me your love;
show me your concern.
But moderate our expectations,
even as we seek your extravagant generosity.
May we live in hope
and hold on in faith,
until the outcome is known
and your peace takes over.
Amen

727 God of purpose and promise,
you take us through the stormy seas of life,
surfing on waves of joy
and plunging into depths of despair.
Be our strong captain
in navigating us through,
and may we ride out the weather,
knowing the calm to come.
Amen

728 Lord of healing and wholeness,
we pray for those recovering from cancer
and those whose treatment is just beginning.
As each person is different and distinct,
so each illness is personal and individual.
May we show our empathy,
not only in our words and wishes,
but also in our practical assistance,
those little unremembered acts
of kindness, love and friendship.
Amen

Coping with suffering

729 Soothing Lord,
remember us as we cope with pain
and strengthen us in our resolve to recover.
You send us the blessing of life,
but also the trial of tough times.
Thank you for the resilience we have
and the patient friendship of family and friends.
Give us the grace to accept what we experience
alongside the hope of deliverance.
Amen

730 All-seeing God,
may we give ourselves to your care,
in partnership with all you have gifted
with medical, nursing and care skills.
May drugs do their work;
may surgeons display their expertise;
and may doctors fulfil their duty of care.
But at the centre of everything,
may we see your bright star,
to ease our pain and see us home.
Amen

731 Dear Lord,
heal us,
strengthen us,
prepare us,
care for us.
And whatever surprises we encounter,
hear us,
comfort us,
enfold us,
give us peace.
Amen

732 Source of light and hope,
give us the strength to cope, in mind and spirit,
with all that life throws at us.
In between the joy and the success,
help us to handle suffering and failure.
May we recognise that we learn more about ourselves
when things go wrong.
Let us respond well and without hesitation
to the suffering of others as well as our own.
Amen

733 God of compassion,
create in us, we pray, the capacity to cope,
in illness, in pain, in heartbreak.
Set our spirits free to lift us up
when our body seems to let us down.
Let faith flower in adversity.
Amen

734 God of gifts and challenges,
you have enabled me to cope with my disability.
Please help others to do so too.
I give thanks that I can access so many things now.
Give me the courage to push back the boundaries further,
to attempt more than I can reasonably expect to do
because you, Lord, through your Son,
made everything possible, made all things new.
Create in us all the yearning to find new things we can do,
but only with your help, God of grace and generosity.
Amen

Worry

735 God of peace and calm,
watch over us in times of struggle,
when everything seems against us,
when we feel we are letting ourselves down
and not doing justice to you.

Take our cares on your broad shoulders
and bring us the focus
to do your will
and cast our worries aside.
Thank you, Lord.
Amen

736 O God who cares,
take our worries and shake them,
so that we see ourselves as we really are.
Take our lives and shake them,
so that we see who you truly are.
May we remain on the one true path
and not be distracted by worries or temptations,
or by the fear of doing wrong,
when we are seeking to do the right thing.
May our risks be your risks, Lord,
so that together we can get things right.
Amen

737 Teaching Lord,
enable us to pray without guilt;
teach us to share without resentment.
Enable us to challenge without fear;
teach us to love without lusting.
Enable us to give without receiving;
teach us to live without worrying.
Enable us to thank without condition;
teach us to follow you without questioning,
enabling Lord.
Amen

738 Heavenly Father,
we pray for the grace you have freely shown
to remove our fears and worries
about the things we cannot change,
about the concerns which you have lifted from us,
about the issues which do not really matter.
But where we face real difficulty,

big decisions and tough times,
help us to discern the right path,
knowing you are with us all the way.
Amen

739 Gracious Lord,
create in us, we pray,
a way to deal with worry
which helps us to face the big issues
without being dragged down by selfish concerns.
Give us the faith in hope to see us through
and the hope of faith to bring us home.
Amen

Debt

740 Redeeming Lord,
you have forgiven our debts to you,
our transgressions and omissions.
May we be equally forgiving of others
as we seek to be true to your Son,
Jesus Christ.
Amen

741 Generous Lord,
keep us as the apple of your eye,
despite our many shortcomings.
Hide us under the shadow of your wings,
even though we let you down.
May we show our hospitality to others,
protection in the storm,
asylum under persecution,
not because they are indebted to us,
but because of our debt to you.
Amen

742 God of grace,
bring us the fruits of your Son's sacrifice,
in all that we are and all that we do.
May debts be cancelled,
not just every seven years,
but each time we glimpse your love,
in the acts of kindness of others
and the overwhelming extravagance
of the gift of your Son.
Amen

743 Loving Lord,
give us the benefit of the doubts we have.
Strengthen our faith in the practice of your grace.
Let the full glory of your gift of creation
always be in our minds,
as we seek to be good stewards of your world,
discharging our great debt to you,
which we can never fully grasp.
Amen

744 God of great generosity,
we your unworthy servants
praise and thank you,
in the way we acknowledge our debt to you,
in the way you have removed that debt,
in the way you encourage us to forgive the debts of others.
Let the river of your extravagance
pour down like silver,
an ever-flowing stream of kindness and love.
Amen

DEATH AND LOSS

Death

745 God of beginnings and endings,
may our deaths be as memorable as our births,
if not for us, then for those around us.
May we not fear the inevitable,
but nor should we hasten it.
Help us to understand that both life and death
are miracles, are natural,
part of your greater scheme of things, Lord.
Give us the fortitude to understand this,
in ourselves as well as in others.
Help us to cope in the process of death,
for you have taken away its sting,
through the love of your Son, Jesus Christ.
Amen

746 Eternal God,
your Son has showed us that sin and death can be conquered.
Strengthen us in our understanding of this last frontier,
so that our minds can comprehend what our hearts tell us:
that beyond the veil lies your peace;
that we will meet our parents and forebears once more;
that we will no longer feel any suffering;
and that we will bask in your closer presence,
all in the knowledge and certainty that your Son taught us.
Amen

747 God of time and place,
may our time here on earth be worthy of you;
and may our legacy be that your creation is not tainted.
We thank you for the life of . . . as we say farewell.
our memories are rich;
our hearts are full;
our loss is great;
and our tears flow.
Let us all take inspiration
from a life well lived,
a family founded on love

and a lasting influence on us all.
We thank you, Lord, and ask for the peace
that only you can give.
Amen

748 Glorious God,
may the death of . . . cause us to step back,
remembering a full life,
grieving a lost life,
hoping for the peace of eternal life.
We pray for those who mourn, including ourselves.
We pray for those who have cared and supported.
We pray for the communities which have lost a member.
And we pray for the friend we had,
who is now in your closer presence
and whom we will see again,
if we are granted a place in your eternal kingdom,
loving Lord.
Amen

749 God of past and present,
may death have no dominion over life.
Bring us to a proper understanding
of the links between,
and the contrasts of,
life and death, presence and absence.
Let fond memories be the bridge
and your love be the link,
always there, but often not perceived.
Open our eyes to the power of the dead
in making our lives fuller,
in giving us hope, even in our grief.
Amen

750 Amazing grace, saving Lord,
give us the capacity to remember the dead,
not with sadness but with gratitude,
not with anger but with love,
not with guilt but with joy.

Just as we are born to die,
so we live that we might be with you,
in this life and in eternal life,
as long as we hold our faith and our nerve,
as you have always held us in the palm of your hand.
Amen

751 Changing and changeless God,
help us to understand death, not fear it.
In celebrating those who have gone before,
may we see into the mystery you have in store.
We want to see again those we have known,
as well as meet those we never knew.
Give us hope that we can do both.
If it is your will, it will be our delight.
Amen

752 Loving Lord,
you know the pain of death,
through the comfort of your Son
and his tears at the death of others.
Bring us your insight and compassion
when we see the effects of death
in ourselves and in others.
Strengthen us to give comfort,
knowing that you are there to hold our hands
and strengthen our hearts.
Amen

753 Father of all,
may we set our sights on you when we feel bereft.
You are our first link with the dead,
not a last resort when all else fails.
Give us encouragement that all is well,
faith that we can carry on,
and trust that the souls departed
are safe in your hands,
loving Lord, saving grace.
Amen

A prayer in memory of . . .

754 Dear Lord,
there is never a day when I do not think of . . . ,
never a family occasion when *s/he* is not there.
I know *s/he* is safe in the peace of your presence,
but I do miss *her/him* being close to me.

I give thanks for *her/his* life,
for what *s/he* meant as a special friend.
Let the fond memories I have stay forever
and take the place of the tears that have been shed.

May the special bonds that we had grow in different ways,
as our past fades and our futures converge.
There is always a special place in my heart for *her/him.*
May *s/he* know the love we feel – and be glad.
Amen

JUSTICE

Courage to do the right thing

755 Patient Lord,
teach us the art of active expectation.
As John the Baptist has shown us the way,
so let the anticipation begin with our repentance.
Then we can tell out the ways of your Son
who brings hope to the poor and needy,
challenge to the rich and powerful.
We pray that we can do justice to your purpose
in our words and deeds, our hearts and minds,
confident that you will lead us in your Spirit of truth.
Amen

756 Strengthen us, we pray, Lord, in our will and ability
to give an account of the hope we have in you.
May we seek always to do what is right in your sight
and to proclaim your name when challenged.
Then let your word flourish and touch our hearts.
Amen

757 Lord of life-giving water and divine authority,
may we always seek out the truth about people
so that we can grow in love for them as they really are
rather than accept the outward show.
You see right into our heart, Lord.
Give us the presence of mind, as well as the warmth of heart,
to acknowledge you and turn away from selfish ambition,
making our joy complete and our journey worthwhile.
Amen

758 Lord of patience,
grant us the insight to know the right time to be patient
and the right time to complain.
Help us to be always aware of the things we need to take
responsibility for,
and those things we need to bring before you
for your guidance and direction.
Let us never seek to usurp your sovereignty

or run away from your oversight.
Thank you, Lord, that you take an interest in our actions
and in our salvation.
Amen

759 Teach us to trust, Lord.
Whatever the problem, however difficult the task,
whenever we feel in danger,
help us to be calm in the knowledge that you are with us.
We know it does not help to worry and panic,
but may we feel in our hearts what we accept in our minds.
And let us be sensitive to others who fear and are yet to trust.
Thank you for your patience, immanent God.
Amen

760 You are the source of all holiness, generous God.
As we wait on you and listen for your call,
grant us the desire, and equip us with the means,
to explore the extent of your love.
We wonder at your Son's healing powers,
the time he gives to every single thing he does,
and the way your gifts to us can be shared with others.
Help us to discern how best we can return
to a proper relationship with you
through the example of others and a love for you.
Amen

761 Lord of our prayers,
hear us as we ask for your saving grace,
for knowledge of the truth through your Son,
and for a glimpse of your kingdom
through the lives and example of saints and martyrs
spanning the ages,
from the first disciples.
Give us the capacity to act in times of trouble,
making the most of the gifts we have received
and turning them to good account in following you.
May all that we do honour you and show the love of your Son.
Amen

The imprisoned and the oppressed

762 God of freedom,
we pray for those in prison,
the justly imprisoned
as well as those without fault,
the victims of injustice.
For those who have transgressed,
may repentance lead to rehabilitation.
For those wrongly sentenced,
may reconciliation remove bitterness.
And let freedom be the prize
for all who have faith in you.
Amen

763 God of justice and mercy,
watch over your servants,
imprisoned by oppression;
caught up in slavery;
trapped in poverty;
kept quiet by censorship;
victimised for their faith;
martyred for their beliefs.
In the restoration of their activities
may their spirits run free,
through the grace of your love,
and the knowledge of your presence.
Amen

764 Sovereign Lord,
friend of the oppressed, guardian of the weak,
bring to your people a new beginning,
so that tyrants change their ways,
sinners look for repentance, victims forgive,
and your perfect peace is found.
Let there be a new heaven and a new earth,
wherever fear and fighting currently stalk the land.
Amen

765 God of grace,
let judgement be in your hands
when we falter and fail
in meeting our responsibilities to you.
And when we let each other down,
through envy, greed and hatred,
may justice be tinged with mercy,
so that wrongdoing is justly punished,
but retribution is left to you,
who knows us better than we know ourselves.
Amen

766 Saviour, Lord,
fill us with a sense of justice,
as we seek to follow the rule of law.
But may we follow the example of your Son,
in challenging unfair laws,
in overturning injustice wherever we find it,
in loving the sinner while condemning the sin,
and in never giving up on humanity.
Just as you saw hope in restoring your relationship with us,
may we recognise hope in the future of prisoners,
salvation through the suffering of your Son,
alongside the criminals on the cross.
Amen

The righteous and the sinner

767 Father Almighty,
you gave us free will
for us to abuse or use well.
Help us to do right
when we want to do wrong.
Let the righteous flourish
as examples to us all,
as your Son was.
Let the sinners see the errors of their ways:
lead them back to you,

with our help,
under your direction,
in love and hope.
Amen

768 God of great expectations,
when we fall short, help us up.
When we don't try, give us 'umph'.
When we overreach ourselves, may we not despair.
Send us out in your name
when we try to take risks for you.
And hold us back from doing harm
when we act selfishly.
Righteous or sinner,
selfless or selfish,
stay with us and keep us on the right path,
loving Lord.
Amen

769 Heavenly Father,
your Son washed away our sins,
but we ask that we remain penitent
for the wrong things we continue to do,
so that we never lose sight of you.
Give us the grace
to understand right from wrong,
but also to love both sinners and righteous,
as your Son showed us on the cross,
as we should do every day,
however hard it is.
Send us out in the power of the Spirit,
to do always what is righteous in your sight.
Amen

770 God of might and right,
have mercy on sinners and saints,
because sinners can become saints,
as you have shown us throughout history.
We remember the transgressions

of David, of Solomon, of Saul.
We remember the faint-heartedness of Peter,
of Thomas, of the young lawyer.
We remember the temptations of Jesus by Satan.
May our failings become our strengths,
like Peter, like Paul,
as Jesus has shown us
in bursting the tomb after the trauma of Calvary.
Amen

771 Lord of all hopefulness,
gather us into your calm waters,
especially when the seas have been rough.
Make us aware of your presence,
even when all seems to be lost.
Give us the strength of your Holy Spirit,
in good times and bad,
so that all the righteous
can be encouraged,
and the wicked can be saved:
through your grace,
through the good will of strangers,
and through the continuous prayers
of religious everywhere.
Amen

Crime

772 God of judgement and forgiveness,
when temptation strikes and people do wrong,
may they soon know the error of their ways
and recognise the hurt they have caused.
And in repaying their debt to society,
may society in turn forgive,
as your Son forgave the criminal on the cross,
so that faith is restored
and restoration can be made.
Amen

773 God of justice,
you set us clear standards
and give us ten commandments.
May those who transgress
know the pain of the victims:
and even where there are no obvious victims
may they realise how they have done harm.
So let rehabilitation replace guilt
and restorative justice overcome hate.
Amen

774 Almighty God,
you have given us an alternative
to selfishness and crime.
May those who have practised evil ways
see that your way is the better way,
that helping yourself harms others,
that using unreasonable force brings needless hurt.
May our justice mirror your judgement,
slow to chide and swift to forgive,
where repentance is clear
and sorrow is genuine.
Amen

775 Loving Lord,
may we live by example,
showing mercy and upholding justice.
Create in society
a desire for community.
Give to communities
a will to make things work,
taking responsibility for developing mutual support,
not fomenting sectarian hate.
Amen

776 God of grace,
we have all done wrong,
not just in words and action,
but in our thoughts and intentions.

Have pity on those who have gone too far
in giving expression to those evil thoughts
and have paid the penalty.
May they be transformed by the experience,
not to be hardened criminals
but to be restored citizens,
faithful to you and good neighbours to others.
Amen

The bully and the bullied

777 Almighty God,
just as you use your power sparingly,
not in anger but justly,
so may we restrain our instinct
to dominate or intimidate.
Give to the bullied resilience,
to the bully restraint,
to the situation peace,
and to the future hope.
Amen

778 Lord of all,
bring your healing to the bullied:
may they regain their confidence.
Bring your mercy on the bullies:
may they see the light,
as you show them the way.
May they know the truth,
as you share the life.
At work, at school, at home,
give us the confidence
to take on the bullies
and care for the bullied.
Amen

779 God of greatness,
show us how to use our power wisely,
not to intimidate or humiliate.
But let us also strive to find
a way to transform the bullies,
turning Goliaths into Davids,
transforming Sauls into Pauls,
changing Herods into Simeons.
Everything is possible
to a God who sends his only Son
to be bullied, killed and resurrected.
Amen

780 Heavenly Father,
look on our feeble efforts to resist evil
and give us strength.
As your Son took on the forces of sin and death –
and won,
so may we be empowered by your Holy Spirit
to battle against injustice,
oppose oppression,
and seek to establish your kingdom,
here on earth.
Amen

781 Essential Lord,
set out for us clear pathways
so that our routes are the right ones.
Help us to recognise blind alleys
and to show the pointlessness of blind rage.
Let our purpose be your purpose
and let us not be deflected
by the desire to dominate others
or to acquiesce in bullying,
whether by individuals or nations.
Let the flame of freedom
be fuelled by your beacon of hope.
Amen

REPENTANCE, MERCY AND FORGIVENESS

782 God of all nations and of all time,
we rejoice that you broke through the limitations of humanity through your Son.
Open our eyes, Lord, to the miracles that faith can bring,
the healing that can come through faith,
and the gateway to the freedom that faith can provide.
You always remain faithful to us.
May we be constant and consistent in our response to you
and ask for forgiveness when we stray from your path.
Amen

783 Merciful Lord,
you do not reject us even when we reject you.
So may we respond to your forgiveness
and your Son's redemption
by renewing our commitment and deepening our faith.
We wonder at your Son's healing power in restoring
the health and wholeness of the Canaanite woman's daughter.
Bring, we pray, to your faithful people
not only pardon and peace, but also the gifts of praise and prayer.
Amen

784 God of peace and love,
may your love drive out the darkness in our hearts,
so that we may be open to your will.
Help us, through the fellowship of others,
and through your Son's forgiveness and loving kindness,
to be witnesses to your truth.
May our strength derive from you and our faith depend on you.
Deepen our understanding, Lord,
through our experience of your grace.
Amen

785 Give us the courage, Lord, to speak up for you,
even in the face of threats and scorn.
This is the least we should be able to do,
in view of your Son's suffering on the cross

to bring salvation and forgiveness to all.
We often know what we should do,
but without the promptings of the Holy Spirit,
we sometimes lack the will.
May we gain our strength and inspiration from your Son's example,
through your grace.
Amen

786 God of forgiveness and justice, who gives us our daily bread;
who watches over us, day and night;
who knows our every need and every failing:
grant us, we pray, the humility and generosity
to show to others the care your Son shows to us.
May we be practical in our faith,
but rooted in the love and understanding we seek
as we grow in the knowledge of you
and in the strength of purpose you can give us
if we only pause, reflect and pray for the Holy Spirit to guide us.
Amen

787 Generous provider,
who provided manna in the desert to the people of Israel,
we give thanks for the bread of life promised by your Son.
May we rejoice that he sought us out for repentance and forgiveness
and has fed the hungry with good things.
Let us show our gratitude not only in our prayers
but also in the way we witness to the truth,
in the way we put into practice what you have taught us,
and in the way we are put to the test.
Amen

788 God of splendour and righteousness,
lift us out of the wilderness into your wonderful light.
Your messenger John showed us the way.
Let us follow his path of repentance for the forgiveness of sins,
so that we can make a new start,

just as you have given your people hope through the new covenant,
providing a straight path for us to follow, willingly and joyfully.
Amen

789 Rock of ages, stay with me, even when I stray from your ways.
Let us never take you for granted and always be open to your call.
Hear our repentance and help us to build on our genuine desire
to do better,
to amend our ways, and to follow you in love and trust,
as your Son showed us.
We are glad that we have a second chance
to restore our relationship with you, generous God.
Lord, in your mercy.
Amen

790 We pray that the faith and love of your Son,
together with the overflowing of your grace,
bring us sinners to repentance and forgiveness
and take us to be the disciples and witnesses
you would want us to be.
We are always in your debt,
but give us the strength and will to repay your trust in us,
both in the way we live and love,
and also in the way we proclaim your name, sing your praises,
gracious God.
Amen

REMEMBRANCE

Remembrance Day/Sunday

791 Generous God,
we give thanks for the sacrifice
of those who gave their lives in war.
We especially remember the allied forces
in two world wars,
as well as those who fell in more recent conflicts,
including the Falklands, Iraq and Afghanistan.
In a moment of silence we remember individuals
amongst our friends . . .
amongst our families . . .
from our community . . .
We salute the bravery that took them far from home
and acknowledge the grief of loved ones back home.
May we always remember;
may we never forget.
Amen

792 God of remembrance,
no one is forgotten in your eyes,
whether they are here on earth
or with you in heaven:
the youngest, the oldest;
the courageous, the timid;
the single person, the family member;
the able, the disabled.
All have played their part in your world
and have a place in your kingdom,
through your grace and their faith.
May we long remember all who went before,
especially those whose lives were cut short through war,
and whose efforts have made the rest of us safer.
We ask this through the one who sacrificed all for us,
Jesus Christ, our Saviour.
Amen

793 Lord of life and death,
give us the hope that your Son brought,
even when it is hard to bear the loss of loved ones.
Give us the promise of eternity for those we see no more.
Give to those who mourn fond memories of life in its abundance.
Create in us all the capacity to be truly grateful
    to those who went before
    to those who fought and died for our freedom
    to those who care for injured service personnel
and to those who remain to guard us now, Lord.
We ask this through our Saviour, Jesus Christ.
Amen

794 God of power and mercy,
we ask for your blessings on our service personnel,
in two world wars,
    in countless conflicts around the world,
    in defence of the realm,
    in peace-keeping missions,
    in support of democracy.
At this time we remember
    those who gave their lives to keep us safe,
    those who were injured in the line of duty,
    the loved ones of the dead and maimed,
over the years, including today.
We ask especially that those we remember
are at peace in your eternal kingdom
and are remembered not just once a year,
but in our hearts and minds throughout the year.
Amen

A Battle of Britain Prayer

795 As we mark the anniversary of the Battle of Britain
we pray for all those affected by that conflict in the skies
above us in 1940:

– for those who died in the defence of freedom
– for those who were injured and those who were bereaved
– for all of us today who owe our liberty, our democracy, our values to those from many nations who brought us victory in the skies.

May we honour the peace that was eventually made possible through the efforts of all our armed forces,
and give thanks for the reconciliation that has brought former foes together.
We pray especially on this day for the RAF, the RAF Association and the RAF Benevolent Fund.
Amen

A Prayer for Battle of Britain Sunday

796 Today we remember and give thanks for
the aircrew and ground support staff
who secured our freedom in the skies over Kent and the south-east.
We mourn the loss of many brave men,
but salute the skills, tenacity and bravery
of those who flew and fought for us.
Let their memory and our liberty
be forever linked;
and may we be grateful in every generation
for the deeds of the RAF in those perilous times
when duty called and victory was won.
Amen

MISSION AND MISSIONS

797 Grant to your Church, Lord,
a commitment to lead us through the wilderness
in hope and expectation of your glorious kingdom.
May the flame of hope be at the heart of our worship,
the power of prayer underpin all our activities
and the practice of mission be our purpose.
We pray that our priests and ministers
uphold and explain the faith
so that we can be better witnesses
to the love you have shown to all believers.
Help us all to have a share in carrying the cross,
as we have all benefited
from your Son's sacrifice for the sake of all.
Amen

798 God of hope that springs eternal,
we pray that our faith is strong enough to enable us
to stray from our comfort zone,
to embrace change and cope with the unexpected.
As the eyes of the Samaritan woman at the well were opened
when your Son put his trust in her,
so may we be the living water of your hope
as we receive his word.
And may we always reach out to others
as you have reached out to us through your Son.
Amen

799 Give to your Church, Lord, the skills for mission
and the heart for healing in a broken world.
Let individuals and communities find comfort
and spiritual sustenance when they seek these out.
May the Church – this church – demonstrate through hospitality
and outreach, that self-giving love we saw so clearly at Easter,
through your Son.
May our confidence grow through inspiration,
our courage develop through grace.
Amen

800 Make your Church like the disciples your Son commissioned to spread the word.
Encourage and empower bishops, priests and deacons
and all ministers in their mission, your mission,
and in their support of each other.
May congregations give backing to those who nourish them,
attention to those appointed by you to be their shepherd.
Amen

801 God of growth,
give us, we pray, the will to do your will,
and the means to carry this out.
In allowing us every opportunity to respond to your call
you have shown your love and we have tested your patience.
May the roots of faith that you have planted in us
bear fruit in our lives and multiply your word.
May we go out in joy and be led back in peace,
confident that you are always there to receive us,
whatever our failings and inadequacies.
Amen

802 We pray for the great mission of your Church
in the hope and contemplation of religious;
in the pastoral presence of ministers;
in the inspirational authority of those who lead worship;
in the day-to-day actions of Christians working in your name.
Help them all to make a difference to people's lives
and to open eyes to the joys of the spiritual life.
May we learn from each other in forging a better relationship with you, our God.
Amen

803 Transforming Lord,
we thank you for the various gifts you have bestowed on us,
some of which we have used, some of which we hide or ignore.
Bring out the best in us, we pray,
to your greater glory and as a blessing to us.
Just as you asked Peter to build your Church,
so enable us to be good disciples.

Please sustain us in our ministry
in accordance with your mission and purpose
and bring us closer to your holy presence.
Amen

804 Heavenly Father,
you have taught us through your Son
to love you, our neighbour and ourselves,
in that order and above all else.
That makes it easy for us to remember
and yet it seems we often forget.
Renew us in our efforts to abide by your command
and to spread your gospel near and far,
drawing on your holiness to ensure a strong foundation.
Amen

805 Send your Church out into the community,
bringing hope and good news to people in their homes,
offering hospitality to those we know and some we don't:
all part of your Son's mission to the Gentiles.
And when people do come to our church,
may the experience be special,
the holiness palpable, the music serene,
and, above all, may people feel that you are here,
ready and waiting, listening and responding, gracious Lord.
Amen

806 Bring to the Church today a full understanding of the mission
that you wish for us.
Entrust our archbishops, bishops and other Church leaders
with a vision for the future and an appreciation of the past,
alongside a responsibility for the present.
Help our own church to play its full part in your purpose
for the community.
Amen

807 Breathe on your Church as a life-giving hope for all people.
May the message of our church leaders
resonate with people's inner needs,
yet clearly coming from your great purpose for us.
Let mission be at the heart of that vision,
as we seek your inspiration in our efforts to carry this out.
We pray that we can attract new Christians,
as people search for truth in your world.
Amen

808 In all the Church attempts for you, trusting God,
may the hope you have for humankind
bear fruit in witness and mission.
Bring forward men and women to test their vocation
and to follow your Son's path in ministry and service.
May those who serve in your Church feel the support
of one another, in their allegiance to your word.
Let revival happen in every generation.
Amen

809 Loving Lord,
you gave us the good seed and the good earth
and we watch and pray, hoe and harvest.
Help us to plant seeds of faith in others
and nurture the growth of our own faith.
May we walk by faith, not just sight,
as we explore the world you have given us
and develop a relationship with you which you offer to us,
even when we let you down.
Prepare us for the harvest, we ask, Lord,
even as we start to grow in our love for you.
Amen

810 Let the teaching of your Church
match the power of your Son's parables,
giving us clear teaching in a way which challenges us
yet leaves us to find the right path guided by the Holy Spirit.
May we not expect to be favoured in the commission you
have for us.

But let us respond with joy at the chance to serve you
in any way that seems right to you
and may we show generosity of spirit in all we do.
Amen

811 May your Church reflect your Son's love for the whole person
so that our lives as Christians can be both active and reflective,
and so enable every member of your Church to fulfil their potential.
Help us to give a high priority to succession planning,
as your Son prepared his disciples for their mission
after his ascension.
Set the Holy Spirit free to amaze us all
in the people chosen to lead and those chosen to be faithful disciples.
Amen

812 We pray for the health and vitality of your Church.
Let the best of the long traditions of Christian service
combine with the vibrancy of new ways of praise and service,
bringing young and old together in worship
and common understanding of your timelessness.
Create in bishops and priests, dioceses and parishes,
the determination to make things happen,
the confidence in each other to grow future leaders
and a real passion for mission and outreach.
Amen

813 Give inspiration and insight to the leaders of your Church
so that what your Son has taught,
our bishops, priests and curates can explain and explore
to our benefit.
Give them the gifts of pastoral care and prophetic preaching
and may all who profess your name
play a part in your mission and purpose:
to churched and unchurched, sinners and sinned against.
Let us not let you down,
remembering the price your Son paid
to wipe away our disobedience.
Amen

814 Trusting God,
it is your wish to set us free
from the bonds that bind us to earthly things.
Set our sights on matters beyond the horizons we can see.
Turn us upside down and inside out
if that is necessary to know and witness to your Son's love.
Give us the strength to cope and the will to grow in faith and hope.
Amen

815 Bring to your Church throughout the world
a dedication to carry out your Son's vision,
to be his hands, eyes, ears and feet,
to heal the sick and care for the infirm,
and to be with those who are poor and those who mourn.
Empower ministers, priests and laity alike to carry out
the mission you gave us through your Son, Jesus Christ.
Amen

816 We ask for your generous and life-giving Spirit
to give your Church a renewed energy in carrying out your mission.
Through the men and women you have chosen,
may your love be better known and your will better understood.
Give to all involved in your Church
a sense of your presence in our community.
In helping us relate to you,
may the Church become more relevant to this generation.
Amen

817 Channel the holiness and the mission of your Church, Lord,
into a witness to the world of how faith can and does make
a difference to the lives of people today.
Let the principles of your Church shine out in our mission
and the practices of the Church reflect your glory.
Create in our church community, we pray, a real sense of hope
and a passion for sharing it.
Amen

818 We pray for your Church worldwide and for our church here in . . .
Send your blessings on worship leaders and pastors, priests and deacons, bishops and archdeacons, as they carry out your purposes in church and community, school and hospital.
Give them, we ask, the stamina and patience
to work with your people and to your glory.
May they bring a glimpse of your kingdom, the hope of salvation, to the churched and unchurched alike.
And may we all be willing helpers in that mission.
Amen

819 We pray for your Church in its outreach to communities
and for its ability to encourage people to worship you with joy.
Grant to our church and benefice an openness
to new ways of expressing timeless truths;
to people who seek us out;
to the community, encouraging visits and dialogue;
to the Holy Spirit to direct our energies.
In all aspects of the great mission your Son gave us,
may we take confidence from those who have gone before
and give confidence to our church leaders of today.
Amen

820 Give to your Church, we pray, the wisdom of Solomon
in tackling the difficult issues of faith in our lives.
Let those who seek to block your path
come up against a Church which knows your mind,
a Church which is strong for you,
a Church which takes risks, as your Son did.
May those with skills and vocation to serve
be called by you to ministry in the Church,
whatever their background and whatever form that ministry takes.
Grant to this church the opportunity to play its full part in mission as well as ministry.
Amen

821 Bring to your Church a clear understanding of your mission for us.
As Moses spoke through Aaron, may you speak through our clergy, giving us hope in our faith and help in our learning.
May the insights they give us
inform our every action, our every thought,
so that our Church walks tall in its place in our community
and our community looks to the Church
for both support and direction,
under your guidance, local and universal Lord.
Amen

822 Let your Church stir and be stirred
in order to do justice to the good news of your Son Jesus Christ.
May we work to forge a unity of purpose
amongst ourselves in this *church/benefice*
and to make common cause with the wider community we serve
in the hope of mission and the service of Christ.
Amen

823 Set your Church on the right course
to bring your kingdom close,
standing firm and holding fast to the ways of your disciples,
and the wisdom of the early Fathers.
May we make the most of the sayings and doings
of saints down the centuries,
and particularly those special to this church . . .
Give us the insight and the understanding
of those who have studied long and hard,
and who have shared their learning
through books and hymns we hear, use and sing today.
May we rejoice in the gift of learning and the art of writing.
Amen

824 Send us out in your name, we pray,
to be witnesses to your mighty power,
disciples of your way and doers of the mission you gave us.
We pray especially for the people and organisations

who take a lead in mission activities,
meeting practical and spiritual needs
in places far and near, on our doorstep and beyond the horizon.
We pray specially for . . .
Give them strength to bring help and inspiration in your name –
and ours.
Amen

DISCIPLESHIP

825 Create in your Church an openness to your words
and a clear sight of where we need to be in our discipleship.
May our ministers bring insight and enthusiasm to our worship
and may we care for them in all we do.
Let grace abound and unity prevail.
Amen

826 Let your Church be your instrument of justice and peace,
praise and worship.
Equip your bishops, priests and ministers to be your apostles,
spreading and supporting discipleship within and beyond our church buildings.
May our mission be your mission, our priorities your priorities,
and our frailties your strength.
Inspire the leaders of every area of church life
to look for you in their tasks and show you in their outcomes.
Amen

827 Lord,
we are sometimes slow to comprehend the full meaning
of the resurrection of your Son,
just as the early disciples took time to adjust to the new dawn.
Like the travellers on the road to Emmaus,
we are full of stories and broken dreams
of 'what might have been',
when we should just believe in what the prophets foretold
and your Son carried out.
We give thanks that the disciples' eyes were opened
and that you have done the same for us.
Let us never take the story of the resurrection for granted,
but wonder and marvel at what has taken place.
Amen

828 Lord, we often seek reassurance that you are still with us,
just like the disciples after Christ's ascension into heaven.
Yet we know that you are indeed with us,
even in the face of roaring lions and evil ways.
Bring us the peace and love that only you can give,

so that we may study, learn and practise
that love which your Son has showed us.
Encourage and develop our spiritual disciplines, we pray, Lord,
so that we can play our full part in your mission.
May we be joyful and glad in sharing your load,
as we wonder at your glory.
Amen

829 Lift the sights of your Church
to reflect the power of your vision, we pray.
Let us catch the flame of your desire for us,
so that we can carry the torch for you in our lives
as well as in our worship.
Free us from jealously guarding our ways of doing things
when they could be improved
and let new approaches in our churches
evolve naturally from our desire to serve you better
and love you more.
Amen

830 May we seek to extend the ministry of welcome and hospitality
in our churches and in our hearts.
Let new and mature Christians alike learn of your love
through Scripture, worship and the peace of your presence.
And may the common bonds of fellowship between churches
show the unity of your purpose through devoted discipleship,
as your Son taught us.
Amen

831 We pray for your Church, for its leaders and followers.
May we all be your disciples, whatever our ministry.
Create in the institutions and structures of the churches
a real willingness to put first the preaching of the gospel,
through word and example, through love and fellowship,
and through selfless actions and thoughtful acts of kindness.
We pray for the churches suffering persecution
under oppressive governments.
May the resilience of Christians be matched by a reciprocal
relaxation by the authorities.
Amen

832 Here we are, Lord, ready to follow you in the footsteps
of your Son, our Saviour.
May we heed your call, remaining faithful in good times
and bad,
seeking always to know your purpose for us.
Create in us the desire to do your will and equip us
with the understanding
of how to carry out our role to help advance your kingdom.
Amen

833 Your disciples built the foundations of the Church
that seeks to serve you today.
Help that Church to be fit for your purpose
and focused on what is needed to deepen faith
and spread the good news.
Help us all to be part of this great enterprise
and enable those in leadership positions to serve you with
integrity
and to inspire us to grow in faith and love.
Amen

834 As children of God,
may we always seek to please you and learn your ways.
You have always been faithful to us;
strengthen our trust in you, Lord, as you reveal to us the
true path of your Son's faithfulness,
even to death on the cross and now in his resurrection.
We see his hands and his feet and give thanks.
Amen

835 Let your Church witness to the transforming power
of the Christian faith,
in this and every generation.
We owe this to you and all those faithful disciples
who have gone before.
Bring inspiration to our words, depth to our thoughts,
and encouragement to our deeds
as we seek to make a difference in your world.
May we collectively, through prayer and worship,
fellowship and hospitality, do together more than we could
as individuals.
Help us to be the body of Christ.
Amen

836 All-knowing Lord,
you see into our hearts and into our minds.
Give us a servant heart and a grateful mind
so that we can seek to act like Jesus,
to be single-minded yet open-minded,
inclusive of all, yet distinctively Christian.
No matter what we face and how we suffer,
keep us on track, Lord, to follow your Son's way,
and to draw near to you, knowing you are on your way towards us.
Amen

837 Let your Church grasp initiatives and opportunities
to spread your word and share your love.
May we all play a part in contributing to church life,
without fear or favour, posture or pride,
being good disciples and great ambassadors
and making a difference in people's lives
by bringing you into their hearts
and joining hands in worship and praise.
Amen

838 O Lord, our God,
you have high expectations of us,
as you want us to do more than follow your commandments.
But just as we know the extent of your love for us,
so may we redouble our efforts to do more for you,
recycling and redistributing the gifts you have given to us,
making sure that following you comes first.
Help us in enabling that ambition to underpin our life,
at home and at work,
always prompting us in our thoughts and actions.
May we never let you down, as you never let us down.
Amen

839 Grant to your Church the skills and nerve
to transform us and change our society
by challenging our values and morals
and giving a lead in both leadership and discipleship.

May all parts of the church, from archbishops to churchwardens,
priests to readers, regular attenders to occasional communicants,
stand together to know you better
and make you better known.
Amen

SCHOOLS AND EDUCATION

(Prayers in this section are designed mainly for use in schools, academies and colleges, but some will be for wider use as churches remember places of learning in intercessions, when special services are held in church on special occasions and when the Church's role in Education is being discussed in meetings.)

New school year

840 Almighty God,
as we begin this new school year, we ask for your blessing on all who study and work here. May those who are new be helped by those who are returning.
May we accept new challenges with eagerness, new risks with courage, and new insights with openness.
Above all, Lord, assist us, in all our learning, to do our best and to grow in understanding of your world.
We ask this through Jesus Christ, our Lord.
Amen

841 Almighty God,
at the start of another year we come together to commit ourselves to our school community; to our learning and playing; and to each other.
Help us to bring forward all we learnt last year
to make the most of our time in this year's class.
Give us the strength and purpose, Lord, to be a good neighbour and a good Samaritan when others around us need our help.
We ask this through Jesus Christ, our Lord.
Amen

New school term

842 Heavenly Father,
as a new term begins, we promise, with your help, to bring new energy to our work at this *school/academy.*

May we always be aware of the needs of others in school and in the local community, including our church.
Help us to listen and learn in our classes; do our very best in our homework; and play our full part in school and class sports.
We ask this in Jesus' name.
Amen

843 Heavenly Father,
thank you for the refreshment that the holidays have brought, for the people we have met and the places we have been.
As we gather again at the start of a new term, give us the energy to do our best, the desire to aim high and the ability to learn from our mistakes.
We pray for our teachers and our parents and ask that you care for them as they care for us.
We ask this in Jesus' name.
Amen

New Headteacher

844 Almighty God,
we ask your blessing on our new headteacher . . .
Give *him* wisdom and strength in the leadership *he* exercises.
May the school, the church and the wider community assist *him* in this role through personal, practical and prayer support.
And may *his* vision be your vision, Lord, as the school begins a new chapter in its history.
We ask this through Jesus Christ, our Lord.
Amen

845 Almighty God,
we give thanks for the arrival of our new headteacher . . .
May *she* feel welcome and at home here at . . . school.
Help *her* to meet your high expectations, Lord, and help

us to show confidence in *her* leadership, renewing our commitment to the school's mission, and encouraging *her* through our support and prayer.
We ask this through Jesus Christ, our Lord.
Amen

New Priest

846 Heavenly Father,
as our new priest starts *his* ministry in this school and this community, we thank you for the gifts and experience *he* brings.
We look forward to *his* presence among us.
Help us to be responsive to *his* efforts to bring us closer to you and to your church, O God.
May *he* feel welcome and at home in our school and may our church be a place of worship, exploration and celebration for pupils, parents, staff and governors.
We ask this in Jesus' name.
Amen

847 Heavenly Father,
we celebrate the arrival of . . . in our school community and in our church.
Give *her* energy, insight and patience in *her* ministry.
May our school play a full part in the church's life and worship and may our new priest always find a warm welcome in the school.
Through *her* words and work help us to know you better, to worship you joyfully and to give thanks for the love you have shown through your Son, Jesus Christ.
We ask this in Jesus' name.
Amen

New Diocesan Board of Education

848 Almighty God,
as our new Board gathers we ask for your strength and purpose to be clearly apparent in our deliberations.
Help each one of us to seek your will as we give direction to our work and the tasks ahead.
Keep us focused and alert; keep us open to the Holy Spirit.
Create in us a willingness to learn from each other, that we may grow your kingdom through our awareness of the needs of the children and families in our diocese,
our educational communities, and our world.
We ask this through Jesus Christ, our Lord.
Amen

849 Almighty God,
we know that every child matters in your sight.
Help us as a new Board to see where we can bring the light of your love to shine on children, families and the work of education in our diocese.
Direct our thoughts, open our minds and empower us to take risks for your sake.
We ask this through Jesus Christ, our Lord.
Amen

New staff

850 Heavenly Father,
we celebrate the arrival of our new staff member(s) . . .
and ask your blessing on their contribution to our *school/academy.*
May they bring new insights and gifts to our school life and may we welcome and support them in this new step in their career.
We ask this in Jesus' name.
Amen

851 Heavenly Father,
we ask for your guiding hand to be extended to our new staff member(s) . . .
Let them flourish here as they become part of our team.
Give them firmness of purpose, generosity of spirit and willingness to listen. Give us the commitment to show hospitality, provide support and offer a Christian welcome.
We ask this in Jesus' name.
Amen

New school

852 Almighty God,
we give thanks for our new school; for all those who planned, designed and built it; and for the vision that sustained the project.
May the learning and the teaching within these walls reflect that vision and your glory. And let us not take for granted our new surroundings, but appreciate them and allow them to enrich this learning community.
We ask this through Jesus Christ, our Lord.
Amen

853 Almighty God,
bring to these new buildings a sense of your presence.
Bring to our hearts a new purpose.
Bring to our learning and teaching a renewed commitment.
We give thanks for the dedication and expertise of all those who have contributed to this project and we ask for your blessing on those who will benefit from this school, now and in the years to come.
We ask this through Jesus Christ, our Lord.
Amen

Prayers for students and staff

854 Lord God,
as students, as staff, we are all learners here.
Give us the energy and enthusiasm
to push back the boundaries of our knowledge,
to grasp new ideas and concepts,
and to extend our vision of the world.
May our commitment to community show itself,
at home and in this *school/academy*.
May we wear our uniform with pride
and may our own faith journey be full of hope.
Amen

855 Heavenly Father,
at this *school/academy* we know that with you
nothing is beyond our reach.
Bring us the hunger to learn
and the thirst to understand.
May we always listen to teachers,
but also challenge ourselves to do better, to help others,
and to grow in mind, body and spirit.
Help us to be a credit to this place,
to our parents – and to you, Lord.
Amen

856 Creator God,
you gave us space and infinity.
May our place of learning and our church
give us a glimpse of both – and a glimpse of heaven too.
Help us to meet our own and others' aspirations for us,
so that we can be good role models,
to younger students, to our community,
to our families and friends.
Let hope and commitment drive us to do our best,
as only the best is good enough for you,
Lord of all.
Amen

At a staff meeting

857 Heavenly Father,
be with us as we meet.
Guide us as we talk.
Stay with us as we plan.
Open our ears as we listen.
Open our eyes to your vision.
We ask this in Jesus' name.
Amen

858 Heavenly Father,
in our meeting, help us to focus on what is important rather than just what is urgent.
May everything we discuss have a bearing on the children in our charge.
Let us never forget that it is both a privilege and a responsibility to play a part in the education of the young.
Grant that we always support each other in that process.
We ask this in Jesus' name.
Amen

At a Governors' meeting

859 God of challenge and change,
as we meet as a governing body,
help us to focus on the important,
so that the detail can take care of itself.
Help us to think beyond the papers
so that we can understand the impact
of what we discuss and what we decide.
Help us, above all, Lord,
to hold the children, the parents and the staff up to you,
in our thoughts as in this prayer.
Amen

860 Almighty God,
may we bring reflection and wisdom to our meeting.
Use our expertise and our judgement, Lord, in directing our contributions.
Let us be listeners more than speakers.
And may we always have in mind your will
for the well-being and the future of the school.
We ask this through Jesus Christ, our Lord.
Amen

861 Almighty God,
we pray for our *school/academy* and our meeting: grant us
the wisdom to conduct our business in a good spirit,
open to the views of others but firm in the purpose of our endeavour, and guided by your will.
May our decisions always support the mission of this school and your church.
We ask this through Jesus Christ, our Lord.
Amen

At a strategy meeting

862 Lord of all,
keep us aware of the big picture
while setting out the small steps.
Bring us reflection before we speak
and wisdom as we plan.
Keep us on the path you have set for us
and help us to discern
our goal and your will.
Amen

At a curriculum committee

863 Creative God,
as we meet to plan and review the curriculum,
help us to draw from experience and evidence

in seeking improvement and change.
Lead us to your truth
through the curriculum we offer at this *school/academy.*
Amen

At a finance and premises committee

864 God of sure foundations,
in our deliberations today,
may we help to ensure secure finances for our *school/academy,*
safe premises for our children and staff
and adequate space, heat and light
to allow the creative flame
to flourish and our school to prosper.
Amen

At a finance committee

865 God who provides,
may our meeting seek to identify the resources needed
for teaching and learning here;
to keep under review the wise deployment of those resources
and be ever on the alert
to seek new sources of funding
for the benefit of all at this school.
Amen

At a headteacher/principal review meeting

866 Lord God,
as we meet to review progress,
let us celebrate what's gone well
and not be afraid to look for ways
to do better where necessary.
Give us open hearts and minds
as we seek your guidance
in coming to a common view
about the best ways forward.
Amen

At a worship committee

867 Almighty God,
as we meet to review our worship,
may we aspire to make that worship special.
You know when we fall short,
so help us to know how to make it worthy of your name,
starting with this prayer,
through Jesus Christ our Lord.
Amen

Pre-interview

868 God of wisdom and choice,
as we meet those you have sent for interview,
help the candidates to show who they truly are,
assist us in bringing out the best in them
and guide us to the right decisions
for the school, for them
and, above all, for you, Lord.
Amen

Before an inspection

869 Lord of judgement and mercy,
as we prepare for our OFSTED/SIAMS inspection,
may your Holy Spirit
fill our hearts and our school,
our worship and our lives,
so that our purpose is clear,
and the inspectors' minds focused
on what is good and right in your sight.
Amen

End of school year

870 Almighty God,
we give thanks for all that has been achieved in our *school/academy* this year.
We remember our successes in competitions, as members of teams and as individuals. We recall the special occasions during the year when we went on visits, took part in a school production, involved visitors and contributed to a fun project.
Let us not forget the new things we have learnt during the year and the friendships we have made.
Prepare us, Lord, for all that the next school year will bring by granting us and our teachers and everyone in our *school/academy* a great holiday.
We ask this through Jesus Christ, our Lord.
Amen

871 Almighty God,
may we look back on the year with pride at the things achieved, awareness of where we have gone wrong, and thanks for all that our teachers and parents have done for us.
We look forward to the holidays, remembering the friends we have made and all the new things we have learnt and experienced.
Bring us back refreshed and ready for all the next year will offer.
We ask this through Jesus Christ, our Lord.
Amen

End of school term

872 Heavenly Father,
we are ready for the holidays. You know, Lord, that we have done our best and learnt a lot. Thank you for the fun we have had and the hard work we have put into this term.
Help us to carry on learning after this short break.
We ask this in Jesus' name.
Amen

873 Heavenly Father,
as we complete another term, we give thanks for this school community, our class, our friends, our teachers, our teaching assistants, our parents and all who support the school.
Bring us back safely next term.
Just as we look forward to the holidays, so may we look forward to returning here to . . . *(school/academy)*.
We ask this in Jesus' name.
Amen

School closure

874 Almighty God,
we give thanks for . . . *(school/academy)*:
for the vision of those who founded it;
for the headteachers and governors who have had charge of it;
for the Church which has supported it;
and for all the children who have been educated here.
We ask that all those who have learned and taught and administered in our school, and the parents who entrusted their children to the school's care will know your lasting love through their time here and will always have . . . *(school)* in their hearts and minds.
We ask this through Jesus Christ, our Lord.
Amen

875 Almighty God,
in the ending of this chapter in our community's history, we give thanks for the education . . . *(school/academy)* has provided for the pupils here.
May all who have learned, taught and worked here be proud of those gifts they have shared and received.
Wherever people move on to, let a little part of . . . *(school)* be carried with them to help them on their way.
We ask this through Jesus Christ, our Lord.
Amen

Retiring teacher/headteacher

876 Heavenly Father,
as we say goodbye to . . . we thank you for *his* tireless work for this school.
We remember the special ways in which *he* has made *his* mark on our *school/academy* and our community – and how *he* has been special to each one of us.
Only you, Lord, know how hard *he* has worked on our behalf.
Bring *him* a long, happy and fulfilling retirement in the knowledge that *he* has carried out your purpose here.
We ask this in Jesus' name.
Amen

877 Heavenly Father,
we celebrate all that . . . has meant to us here at . . . (school):
in the classroom, in the hall, in *her* office, on the playing field, and also in the community.
Thank you, Lord, for the special gifts *she* has shared with pupils and staff over . . . years at this *school/academy.*
Bring *her* happiness and good health in retirement,
fond memories of this place and a sure knowledge of firm friendships made and a job well done.
We ask this in Jesus' name.
Amen

Retiring/leaving priest

878 Almighty God,
we thank you for the ministry of . . . in our *school/academy.*
As we say farewell to *him* we remember the many ways in which *he* has supported the school, leading worship at our assemblies, making us feel at home in the church, and being available in good times and difficult times.
May . . . continue to serve you, Lord, in your church,
knowing that *he* leaves us firmer in our faith and with a closer relationship with you.
We ask this through Jesus Christ, our Lord.
Amen

879 Almighty God,
we are grateful that you sent . . . to this *school/academy*
and this community to be our pastor and our friend.
We celebrate *her* ministry amongst us as we say farewell
to *her* (and *her* family).
Through her we got to know you better, Lord.
May the link between the school and the church continue
to flourish, building on the firm foundations which you have
laid here through the ministry of . . .
Bestow your blessings on *her* in the next stage of *her* work
in your service.
We ask this through Jesus Christ, our Lord.
Amen

Staff leaving

880 Heavenly Father,
we give thanks for the contribution that . . . has made
to the life of this *school/academy.*
As we say farewell, we remember all that *he* has meant to us
previously, all that *he* has done for the school as a whole,
and *his* contribution to the wider community.
As *he* moves on from this school, Lord, may *he* be aware of
your love in all his future endeavours.
We ask this in Jesus' name.
Amen

881 Heavenly Father,
we will miss . . . in our *school/academy.*
We will miss all the things that make them special:
her sense of humour,
his. . .
We will laugh when we remember
her big earrings,
his odd socks.
Please, Lord, look after them when they leave,
and may they have many good memories of us too.
We ask this in Jesus' name.
Amen

Governor leaving

882 Almighty God,
as . . . steps down from being a governor here, we celebrate *his* commitment to this school during the past . . . years.
You know, Lord, the late hours and many days *he* put in and you know the difference *he* has made.
In asking for your blessing on *him* we also ask for your continued inspiration in the work of governors in the years to come.
We ask this through Jesus Christ, our Lord.
Amen

883 Almighty God,
we will miss the contribution . . . has made to our deliberations, our decisions and our debates.
We ask, Lord, that you will continue to use *her* ministry in other ways to extend your kingdom.
We thank you for *her* lasting legacy to our *school/academy* and our community.
May *her* contribution be an indication of our desire to serve you always.
We ask this through Jesus Christ, our Lord.
Amen

End of day

884 Heavenly Father,
we offer you our day's work.
As we prepare to go home, help us to reflect on what we have learnt, what we have seen, what we have said, what we have struggled with, and what we have enjoyed.
We are sorry for any angry words or unjust actions.
We thank you, Lord, for the whole day and look forward to what tomorrow will bring.
We ask this in Jesus' name.
Amen

885 Heavenly Father,
thank you for our school day.
Thank you for revealing more of your world to us.
Thank you for all the experiences this day has brought.
May our school always be a learning community with you as its focus, Lord.
Give us rest tonight so that we can return refreshed and ready to resume our studies.
We ask this in Jesus' name.
Amen

Leavers' service

886 Almighty God,
we ask for your blessing on all who are moving on to their next school.
We give thanks for what they have contributed to this school, what they have learnt and what they have left behind them.
May they be a credit to our school in all that they achieve in their future lives and may they remain grateful for what this school has given them.
We ask this through Jesus Christ, our Lord.
Amen

887 Almighty God,
we thank you for the achievements and hard work of all those who are leaving this term; for the friendships they have made; for the service they have given.
We ask, Lord, for your protection and inspiration as they move on to the next step in their education, the next development of your purpose for them.
May they remember the Christian values they have learnt in this school and may they always follow your ways.
We ask this through Jesus Christ, our Lord.
Amen

Further and higher education

888 Heavenly Father,
may this college serve the surrounding community in ways which draw together the skills and needs of its people.
Give ambition to students, energy to lecturers and vision to managers of this institution.
May the culture of dedication among staff be reciprocated by a respect for learning among students.
We ask, Lord, that vocational pathways are found
and are well travelled in this place,
in Jesus' name.
Amen

889 Heavenly Father,
we give thanks for the staff and students in this *college*, the gifts they bring, the strengths they share
and the friendships they make.
Bring a spirit of openness and integrity to the teaching and learning that goes on here.
And may the wider community benefit from the skills, knowledge and judgement available at this institution.
We ask this in Jesus' name.
Amen

890 Almighty God,
we ask for your blessings on . . . *college*.
Bring us the wisdom to make the most of the learning experience, whether listening and observing, or sharing and doing.
May the focus of our education be excellence and service.
May the fruits of our work here promote lifelong learning in mind, body and spirit.
And may our college be a force for creativity, quality of life and care in our community.
We ask this through Jesus Christ, our Lord.
Amen

891 Heavenly Father,
renew, refresh and regenerate the love of learning
in this *university.*
May research into truth flourish here.
Inspire hearts and minds to thirst after knowledge
and to use wisdom in its application.
Let debate illuminate, not obfuscate.
May justice underpin scholarship.
We ask this in Jesus' name.
Amen

892 Heavenly Father,
we pray that this place of scholarship and academic
endeavour may continue to challenge and surprise us,
just as your Son still does.
May friendships survive argument and debate.
Bring rigour and humour to life at our university, but let us
also draw from the well of divine spirituality that you have
provided for us, extravagant God.
We ask this in Jesus' name.
Amen

893 Almighty God,
make this *university* a place where truth is pursued
and you are found.
May minds be stretched and knowledge extended.
Help us to know ourselves better as we debate and write,
test and experiment.
May tutors and those they teach never cease to surprise
and be surprised.
And never let us forget that we are stewards of a world
that you have created.
We ask this through Jesus Christ, our Lord.
Amen

894 Almighty God,
we give thanks for the ministry and mission of . . . ,
as *s/he* retires as Vice Chancellor/Principal of . . .
May we rejoice with *him/her* at the achievements of our higher education communities:
students and staff, researchers and lecturers, leaders and learners.
Let us pray that freedom to explore and question
may remain a bulwark of our society and our faith.
And may the search for truth
lead us to the way of all truth,
your Son, our Saviour, Jesus Christ.
Amen

School amalgamation

895 Heavenly Father,
as our two schools come together, please bless our new creation.
May we become stronger as we grow larger.
May we care for each other and share what both our schools have.
Above all, Lord, may we know you better through our worship together.
We ask this in Jesus' name.
Amen

896 Heavenly Father,
as we now become . . . *(school/academy)*, help us to respect our different origins.
May we learn to think of ourselves as one community;
our teachers, teaching assistants and support team as one staff; and our *school/academy* aims as one shared vision.
Bring unity and purpose to our work and learning.
We ask this in Jesus' name.
Amen

Federation of schools

897 Almighty God,
create in us the will to work together and give us the means to collaborate effectively; enable the gifts of both our schools to flourish in our wider school community.
May your name be honoured and your Son's example followed in all that we do individually and together.
We ask this through Jesus Christ, our Lord.
Amen

898 Almighty God,
bring to us new insights and new ways of working together.
May our schools bring to each other new opportunities for learning and growing forward together.
We ask that the collaboration we seek provides the challenge and change you ask of us all, through your transforming love.
We ask this through Jesus Christ, our Lord.
Amen

Opening of new school buildings

899 God of purpose and understanding,
we ask for your blessings on our new school,
on all the teaching and learning that happens in this place,
and on the people who work and study here.
May this beautiful building
reflect your glory.
May this wonderful setting
remain in our imagination.
And may we never forget
the skills, perseverance and perspiration
that turned this vision into a reality for the community,
through the grace of your Son, Jesus Christ.
Amen

900 Heavenly Father,
may this new building be an extension of your kingdom,
a passport to new learning opportunities and a focus
for excellence.
Help us to integrate what it can offer into the fabric
of the school/academy.
Inspire all those who use it with your purpose for them.
In sharing these facilities may the school and the community
grow ever closer.
We ask this in Jesus' name.
Amen

901 Heavenly Father,
with this new building to inspire us, set our sights high.
With you as our guide, help us to enrich the education
that goes on in this place.
May many people benefit from the new facilities and may
skills learnt here reflect the skills which went into
the building's design and construction.
We ask this in Jesus' name.
Amen

New day

902 Almighty God,
as our school day begins, we meet to dedicate ourselves
to you.
May our hopes for today reflect your hopes for us.
Help us to face the challenges and take the opportunities
that this day brings.
And in a moment of silence let us prepare ourselves
for the tasks ahead . . .
Be with us, Lord, in all that we do and say, and give us
the time for reflection on our learning.
We ask this through Jesus Christ, our Lord.
Amen

903 Almighty God,
may this new day bring light as well as heat; help to overcome the hurdles; fun alongside the struggles.
Help us to put things in perspective, not to rush to judgement, and to listen hard to what others are saying.
May this school be a real learning community today.
We ask this through Jesus Christ, our Lord.
Amen

Education Sunday

904 Almighty God,
as we celebrate all that education can offer us and all that we can bring to education, we give thanks for the role of the church in our schools and the contribution of schools to the life of our church.
Help those who teach and those who learn to build on these links.
Grant wisdom to governors of schools and to PCC members, to diocesan and council officers, and to national government in sustaining and developing the educational system in all its depth and breadth.
And in their growth of understanding and knowledge, may all pupils seek to love you, as you love them.
We ask this through Jesus Christ, our Lord.
Amen

905 Almighty God,
on this special Sunday we pray for the schools, academies and colleges we serve.
May those who study prosper and grow in their learning.
Enable those who teach, support, administer or govern to carry out their duties with commitment and energy, knowing they have the support of this congregation through our prayers and in our actions.
Show us, Lord, new ways of expressing and developing the church's partnership with our schools and colleges.
We ask this through Jesus Christ, our Lord.
Amen

Significant school anniversaries

906 Heavenly Father,
as we celebrate the school's . . . years of service to our community,
we give thanks for those who have learned about you here;
those who have grown in faith here and those
who have made . . . a special place.
May the staff and governors, parents and pupils
always value their time and each other's efforts at
this *school/academy*.
May they look back in appreciation and forward in hope.
Give to this learning community the confidence
to make a difference,
to challenge what is wrong
and champion what is right,
and to grow daily in our love for you.
We ask this in Jesus' name.
Amen

907 Heavenly Father,
on this special day for the *school/academy* we give thanks for all those who have contributed to the life of this place.
Thank you for the commitment of the people who founded the school and for all the teaching and learning that has taken place here.
We ask that your Church continues to provide us with support and prayer, inspiration and love.
We ask this in Jesus' name.
Amen

908 Almighty God,
it's a great day.
Please be with us as we celebrate and have fun.
Help us to value what we have and not worry about what we don't have.
Thank you for all those who have built up our *school/academy*
And the community around us,
and we ask you to bless everyone in our *school/academy* today.
We ask this through Jesus Christ, our Lord.
Amen

909 Almighty God,
it is only . . . years since we became . . . *(school/academy).*
We have enjoyed the journey so far and we look ahead
with confidence and expectation.
Be with us on our journey, in our church,
in our community, in our *school/academy* and in our hearts.
We ask this through Jesus Christ, our Lord.
Amen

New birth for staff members

910 Heavenly Father,
as we welcome back our (head)teacher we celebrate the
arrival of their child. We thank you for the gift of a new life
and ask that the family of this school be an extension
of their own.
Bring happiness and a bright future to . . .
We ask this in Jesus' name.
Amen

911 Heavenly Father,
as we celebrate the arrival of a new brother/sister for . . .
we pray for all newborn babies around the world.
In these early weeks of life, bring renewed efforts to all who
care and protect the newborn.
May love combine with nursing and medical care to
safeguard their health.
May adequate nourishment be available wherever it is
needed and not just where it is wanted.
May hope overcome adversity.
We ask this in Jesus' name.
Amen

Inspection reports

912 Almighty God,
as we receive and celebrate our school's inspection report(s),
we acknowledge and give thanks for all the hard work
represented and recognised in the report(s).
You know, Lord, the strengths of this school community.
You know our weaknesses too.
May we go forward together in confidence and in faith
so that we can continue to be worthy of your purpose.
We ask this through Jesus Christ, our Lord.
Amen

913 Almighty God,
great news!
We pray that these reports are read and valued by staff,
governors, parents and pupils and recognised as part of your
'good news' too, Lord.
Help all those in our community to see our *school/academy*
as we really are and to support us in all our activities.
May we continue to grow as a learning community.
And may your church be at the heart of our school life.
We ask this through Jesus Christ, our Lord.
Amen

Speech/prize day

914 Heavenly Father,
today we celebrate achievement.
But we know, Lord, that our efforts are in vain without you.
So we give thanks for all the opportunities that this *school/academy* has provided, the dedication of the staff and the support of our parents.
As we applaud the excellence and service of the prizewinners
we remember the progress we have all made
and, in a moment of silence, we bring before you our own
special memory of an achievement this year . . .
May all we do be offered to you, Lord.
We ask this in Jesus' name.
Amen

915 Heavenly Father,
every person is special in your sight.
We know that this *school/academy* is also special to you, Lord.
Let today be a celebration of achievements for individuals and teams, but also a celebration of the life of this *school/academy* and its place in our community.
We give thanks for the hard work of teachers, support staff and governors which has enabled us all to give our best,
to learn from each other and to serve you.
In applauding the prizewinners may we also applaud you, Lord.
We ask this in Jesus' name.
Amen

Different faiths

916 Almighty God,
as we gather as people of faith, we thank you for
the different paths we have been given to follow;
the different ways in which we can worship you;
the different ways we have experienced your love.
In our lives and in our minds, may we remain true to you
and respectful of each other's different contributions;
may we always be aware of, and celebrate,
the rich diversity of your world.
Amen

917 Loving God,
bring to us an understanding of different cultures and different faiths.
Help us to recognise what binds us together as human beings, what divides us through background and history,
and what we can do to understand each other better.
May we push back the limits of our learning,
knowing that there are no boundaries in your creation.
Amen

918 Lord God,
in our learning about different religions,
help us to hold on to what we believe
and reach out to explore and celebrate what is new.
May we respect the views and beliefs of others.
Create in us, Lord, the capacity to understand and reflect.
Help us to learn fresh ways of being still and knowing that you are God.
Amen

919 Lord God,
on this day when the festival of . . . is celebrated, we thank you for the richness of cultures and religions in your world.
We pray especially for all those in our community and all those worldwide for whom this is a special day.
You gave us all the gift of hospitality. Let us offer and receive that gift as we celebrate and give thanks.
Amen

Disasters and setbacks

920 Almighty God,
help us to understand what has happened, Lord.
Give strength to those who are still suffering – the homeless,
the hungry, those who have lost loved ones,
those who have lost the will to live.
Show your love to them, give them hope and show us
the way to help.
We ask this through Jesus Christ, our Lord.
Amen

921 Almighty God,
we do not know why this disaster has struck . . .
You know all those who have been hurt. You know all those who have been killed. You know all those who are still missing. We pray especially for anyone we know who has been affected; give us the insight to find the ways in which

our school can be of assistance.
Meanwhile we pray for the rescue services and we hope for speedy recovery.
We ask this through Jesus Christ, our Lord.
Amen

922 Heavenly Father,
we pray for our school community at this difficult time.
Help us to recover and rebuild our confidence.
Give strength to our teachers and governors as they meet the challenges ahead.
May pupils and parents join them in preparing for a better future.
Make us proud in our *school/academy* and in all the people who contribute to our learning community.
We ask this in Jesus' name.
Amen

923 Heavenly Father,
help us to come to terms with . . . that has hit our *school/academy* so hard.
Give us the help and the hope from all around to put us back on our feet.
We put our trust in you, Lord, to bring out the best in us at this time.
May our neighbours in this community act as good neighbours and may we repay them by redoubling our efforts in all that we do.
We ask this in Jesus' name.
Amen

Failures and forgiveness

924 Almighty God,
we admit our many failures before you, Lord,
and before each other.
You know the difference between failure without trying
and failure despite trying hard.

We know you are a forgiving God. Forgive our shortcomings and help us to learn from the things we do wrong or do badly.
We ask this through Jesus Christ, our Lord.
Amen

925 Almighty God,
bring us to realise our faults and our failures, we pray.
In a moment of quiet let us think of one thing we have done wrong and for which we are very sorry . . .
Give us and our families and friends a new spirit of support, love and forgiveness.
Help us not to be selfish and to respect others, however difficult that sometimes seems.
We ask this through Jesus Christ, our Lord.
Amen

Death of a pupil/student

926 Heavenly Father,
we give thanks for the life of . . . ; for the smiles, the fun and the friendships *she* brought to our lives.
Through our tears we ask, Lord, that as *she* is welcomed into your loving arms *she* also stays in our hearts.
She will always be special to . . . *school/academy* and to . . . church.
Help us all, family, friends and community, to say farewell to . . . but never to forget *her*.
We ask this in Jesus' name.
Amen

927 Heavenly Father,
at present we can only feel the loss of . . .
We want to be strong and we want to understand why *he* is no longer here with us.
We pray that . . . is safe in your arms, in your heavenly kingdom.
Help us to remember what *he* meant to us and what

he left behind – the laugh, the smile, the favourite comment, the things *he* struggled with.
Bring us happy memories in the tears.
Bring *him* the peace only you can give, Lord of love and mercy.
We ask this in Jesus' name.
Amen

Death of a teacher/headteacher

928 Almighty God,
you know that it will be difficult for us at . . . *school/academy* without . . .
Bring us the strength and the hope to carry on, as *he* would have wished.
We thank you, Lord, for the special gifts *he* brought to this school and shared with us.
May the church and the wider community give thanks for *his* contribution to the life of . . . *(village /town)*
and may we redouble our own efforts to serve each other, in honour of *his* memory.
We ask this through Jesus Christ, our Lord.
Amen

929 Almighty God,
as we remember all that . . . has meant to us at . . . *school/academy,* we pray that *she* is now at peace with you in your eternal kingdom.
Only you know why *she* was taken from us at this time, but we give thanks for *her* special place in our hearts at our school.
We pray for *her* family and friends at this difficult time.
Show your love for them and for us as we struggle to cope with the loss.
May your church be a comfort and a strength to us all.
We ask this through Jesus Christ, our Lord.
Amen

For intercessions at Sunday services

930 Almighty God,
inspire those who exercise their vocation as teachers, lecturers, governors, support staff or helpers.
In our community we pray especially for . . . and for the place(s) of education with which we have a personal link.
Grant wisdom to all who are responsible for education planning, teacher training and policy making.
We pray also for the work of our chaplains that their ministry may be sustained and upheld.
In our wider community we pray for our local authority and for the Diocesan Board of Education.
We ask this through Jesus Christ, our Lord.
Amen

931 God of Hope, may your light guide our educational path.
God of Hunger, may we feed on your wisdom and thirst for your truth.
God of Healing, may you bring learning out of failure, humility from success.
God of Help, may we be a good Samaritan to others.
God of Habit, may we grow in faith and devotion.
We ask this through Jesus Christ, our Lord.
Amen

932 Heavenly Father,
we give thanks for the many opportunities for learning in our schools and community.
We pray for our junior church, for the uniformed organisations and for the mother and toddler group.
We ask for your blessings on those recently confirmed or planning to be confirmed.
We thank you that we have the responsibility and legacy of our church *school/academy*, where excellence and faith can go hand in hand, Lord.
Inspire us all to use our particular
skills in the educational institutions in our community.
We ask this in Jesus' name.
Amen

933 Heavenly Father,
we pray for all pupils and students; we give thanks
for the window on your creation that their education provides,
for the horizons that are in their reach and for the
foundations of wisdom.
Give them the power to reflect on the source of all
knowledge.
Help our nurseries, schools, colleges and universities
to provide a framework for lifelong learning.
We pray especially for headteachers and principals.
We ask this in Jesus' name.
Amen

At a synod

934 Almighty God,
may our synod today bring enlightenment to the
educational issues being debated.
Help us to honour the gifts of learning and teaching
as we discuss the process of education.
Let us be alert to opportunities for the church to bring
wholeness and hope to our places of learning through the
work of Christian teachers and governors, staff and pupils,
priests and laity.
Give direction to our efforts, Lord, and purpose to our
decisions, so that we can make a difference to education
in our diocese.
We ask this through Jesus Christ, our Lord.
Amen

935 Almighty God,
as this synod debates the church's stake in education,
help us to focus on the example of your Son as teacher:
challenging, explaining and clarifying.
In our differing perspectives on the mechanics of education,
let us hold fast to the importance of setting the spirit free
in all our learning communities.

Help us to be creative and thoughtful as we seek to discern
your will for our work.
We ask this through Jesus Christ, our Lord.
Amen

At a PCC meeting

936 Heavenly Father,
inspire us with your wisdom.
School us in your knowledge.
Educate us in your ways.
May our discussions help to bring your kingdom nearer
and make our purpose clearer.
Show us how education can help to reveal your glory.
We ask this in Jesus' name.
Amen

937 Heavenly Father,
as we discuss our relationship with the schools, academies
and colleges in our parish, we pray for all those involved
in education.
Help us to consider ways in which we can assist in
fulfilling your high expectations of schools and pupils,
colleges and students.
May we be ever present, as your representatives, to celebrate
success and to console in difficult times.
Strengthen our church in its mission to support the places
of education in our community.
We ask this in Jesus' name.
Amen

At a Board of Education

938 Almighty God,
we pray for the schools, academies, colleges and universities
in this diocese.
In our deliberations today help us to seek ways

to strengthen your presence in all the institutions we discuss.
May our policies reflect your wisdom, our priorities be true
to your word and our decisions carry your authority.
Let us always be mindful of the legacy of our predecessors
and the long-term consequences of our actions.
We ask this through Jesus Christ, our Lord.
Amen

939 Almighty God,
we are guardians of your church's role in education,
especially in our church schools.
Help us to do all in our power, under your guidance,
to discuss the issues before us with the care, rigour
and thought we would expect in our places of learning;
let us not fall short of your high expectations in our policy
and decision-making.
We pray especially for schools and their churches facing
particular challenges at this time, and for the work of this
Board and its staff in giving appropriate support.
We ask this through Jesus Christ, our Lord.
Amen

Education and the national/worldwide Church

940 Almighty God,
guide your Church nationally to stay true to the vision that
inspired the development of education in this country.
Help us to remember our responsibilities to those in our
schools, academies, colleges and universities and to rekindle
the creative flame of our imagination in planning for future
generations.
In reaffirming our faith in the future, be with us in the
challenges ahead, prepare us for the celebrations and the
setbacks, and above all, Lord, give us a glimpse of the
breadth, length, height and depth of your love.
We ask this through Jesus Christ our Lord.
Amen

941 Almighty God,
we pray for the churches and schools across the world
linked to us through the *Anglican Communion.*
We thank you for all those who have spread your word in lands far and near.
Make us open to learning about and learning from Christians in all parts of the world.
We especially pray for schools and colleges in . . .
We ask this through Jesus Christ our Lord.
Amen

(The prayers which follow are meant to be models of what could be a school's own prayer, said regularly and on special occasions. However, they can also be used as 'one off' prayers in daily worship.)

Primary school/academy prayer

942 Almighty God,
may our school be welcoming.
May our school be encouraging.
Let friendship flourish here.
Let learning fill our day.
Give us the strength to do our best.
Give us the hope to carry on.
Be our guide in all we do.
Lord, make this school your home too.
We ask this through Jesus Christ, our Lord.
Amen

943 Almighty God,
we give thanks for our *school.*
For us it is a special place.
Make it special for you, Lord, and bring your peace,
love and friendship to everything we do here.
As we learn and as we play, may we always be in your safe keeping.
We ask this through Jesus Christ, our Lord.
Amen

944 Heavenly Father,
be with us in our learning.
Be with us in our playing.
Be with us in our laughter.
Be with us in our tears.
Be with us when we get things right and when we get things wrong.
Be with us as we come to school and when we travel home.
We know that you will always be here for us, Lord,
at . . . *school.*
We ask this in Jesus' name.
Amen

945 Heavenly Father,
help our learning and our knowing and bring us friendship and fellowship.
Take us to new places, Lord, as our teachers show us
the wonders of your creation.
May we help each other at . . . *school* so that we
can learn from everyone around us.
We pray also for our families and our homes; keep them safe while we are safe at school.
We ask this in Jesus' name.
Amen

Secondary school/academy prayer

946 Almighty God,
we pray for this school and all who contribute to its achievements as a place of learning.
Bring a sense of purpose to our work, a commitment
to justice in our behaviour and a desire for integrity
and wholeness in our being.
May we succeed with each other's help rather than at each other's expense.
May our ambitions for ourselves embrace your ambitions for us, Lord.
And may this school be a Christian presence in the wider community.
We ask this through Jesus Christ, our Lord.
Amen

947 Almighty God,
help us to grow forward together in faith and fellowship.
Grant that both our worship and our work at this *school*
reflect your purpose for us.
Help us to share our strengths and to learn from others
as we try to overcome our weaknesses.
Bind us into a community, with you at the centre
of our mission.
May this school be a beacon of hope and a source
of inspiration under your guidance.
We ask this through Jesus Christ, our Lord.
Amen

BIDDING PRAYERS AND BLESSINGS

Advent Sunday

Bidding Prayer

948 From darkness to light,
from expectation to fulfilment,
may our service reflect our hopes
and the sureness of your promise.
May we all, with John,
be forerunners for the birth of your Son,
as we celebrate the start of Advent today.
Amen

Blessing

949 As we begin our preparation for the coming of the Lord,
let the expectation bring hope;
let the waiting bring joyful anticipation;
and let the season of Advent bring prayerful reflection.

And may the blessing . . .

Christmas

Bidding Prayer

950 God of hope,
lead us to your Son,
as we remember his birth.
Lead us to better ways,
as we follow his way.
Lead us to watch and worship,
as the shepherds show us.
Lead us to celebrate in song,
as we hear the music of the angels.
Lead us to the stable with the animals,
as we join Mary and Joseph,

and the baby in the manger.
May the star of Bethlehem
shine brightly in our lives
and draw us in.
Amen

Blessing

951 Almighty God,
we ask for your blessings
and offer you our thanks,
as Christmas once again enters our lives and hearts.
May the birth of your Son
bring gladness and neighbourliness,
even where there is hardship and hurt.
May our actions and thoughts
reflect the generosity of the gift of your Son, Jesus Christ,
to a world in need of your love.

And may the blessing . . .

Mothering Sunday

Bidding Prayer

952 Today we remember our Mother Church,
Mary, the mother of Jesus,
and our own mothers.
May this service be a time of thanksgiving,
of special memories, of love.
May the protection and nurture of mothers
be celebrated and remembered;
and may we offer our praise to you
for all that motherhood means.
Amen

Blessing

953 As we have given thanks for mothers and motherhood,
may we resolve to renew
our respect for mothering in all its forms;
and to show our gratitude
in acts of kindness and love,
as your Son showed us.

And may the blessing . . .

Easter

Bidding Prayer

954 Alleluia! Christ is risen!
As we celebrate the fact and the deed,
in our service let us remember the sacrifice,
alongside the joy that we feel.
Let us join the angels and the whole heavenly host
in singing songs of praise and celebration,
welcoming your Son, our Saviour,
Jesus Christ, risen from the dead
and giving us all a new start.
Amen

Blessing

955 May bells ring out and music sound
to spread the news that Christ is risen
so that the world may know
the saving grace of the risen Lord.

And may the blessing . . .

Pentecost

Bidding Prayer

956 Come, Holy Spirit, join our service today.
May we feel the winds of change,
as the disciples did.
May we feel refreshed and reborn
to sing your praises;
to share your word;
to spread the good news;
in the sure and certain knowledge of your love for us.
Amen

Harvest

Bidding Prayer

957 As we gather to celebrate the fruits of the earth,
let us also remember the fruits of the Spirit.
May our gifts today
remind us of your gifts to us,
not just today, but every day.
Let our prayers reflect your wonderful harvest
and let our love for one another
be reflected in the bread and the wine
that reminds us of your love for us,
through your Son, our Saviour.
Amen

Blessing

958 May the abundance of the harvest
always remind us of your extravagance
in creating more than enough for us to eat and drink.
Let the one who gave us the bread of life
give us the resolve to share these gifts with those in need.

And may the blessing . . .

Remembrance

Bidding Prayer

959 As we gather to remember the fallen,
let us give thanks for the sacrifice,
in our prayers, in our silence,
and in our memories of loved ones lost in war.
May our songs and hymns
reflect and do justice to the stories of courage and resistance
in the face of danger and aggression.
And in our service let us take comfort
from the words of love and consolation,
knowing that your Son grieves for them too
and that they are now safe in your heavenly kingdom.
Amen

Blessing

960 Give us the capacity to hope,
even as we mourn those who have fallen.
Give us the comfort to trust
that those who died are now at peace with you.
And give us the generosity of spirit
to mark the sacrifice of all who have died in war,
on every side.

And may the blessing . . .

Healing and wholeness

Bidding Prayer

961 God of healing and wholeness,
be with us as we share our worship,
joined by a common concern for sufferers.
Let us give thanks and praise.

Let us seek healing and hope.
Let us remember and look forward.
We pray this in the name of your Son,
Jesus Christ.
Amen

Blessing

962 May the Father who knows us,
the Son who loves us,
and the Spirit who keeps us whole
give us peace, keep us from harm,
and take way any hurt or despair.

And may the blessing . . .

At a pet service

Bidding Prayer

963 Lord of all creation,
you have brought us together today,
just as you have created our world.
As we prepare to hear and affirm your creatures,
let us remember pets we have known,
the love they have given us
and the love we have shown to them.
And may we now ask
that the pets with us today
share in our worship
and respond to your love.
We ask this in the name of your Son, our friend,
Jesus Christ.
Amen

Blessing

964 So let the birds of the air flourish,
the animals not go hungry,
and the waters show your bounty.

And may the blessing of God Almighty,
the Father, the Son, and the Holy Spirit,
be among *you/us* and all *your/our* pets
and remain with *you/us* always.
Amen

GRACES

965 Lord,
this food and drink you give to us;
our praise and thanks we give to you.
Amen

966 Almighty God,
bless this food
as we break this bread.
Bless this place
as we share our meal.
Bless us all
as we enjoy the fruits of your creation.
And before we eat and drink
we give thanks to you, Lord of all.
Amen

967 Heavenly Father,
as we eat our food
may we sing your praise.
As we lift our glasses
may we offer you our thanks.
As we share our thoughts
may we think of our neighbour.
As we enjoy the plenty before us
may we remember the hungry around us,
as your Son asked us to do.
Amen

968 Lord Almighty,
as we give you thanks for this meal,
may we show thanks in our lives.
Bless the food before us, we pray,
and all who helped to bring it to us today.
Amen

969 Abundant God,
as you fill us up with good things,
make us grateful for the small things.
Open us up to your will and bring us all to your feast.
And as we eat together
may we never forget those who prepared this food,
those who cooked it
and those who do not have fair shares
of the abundance of your creation.
Amen

970 Father of all,
thank you for feeding us;
thank you for needing us.
Bless those who serve
and those who conserve.
And let us be sharers as well as carers
as we enjoy this meal.
Amen

971 Lord,
may this food do us good;
may this drink make us think!
And let us be grateful for this plateful.
Amen

972 Almighty God,
we give thanks for this food: for those who grew it;
for those who brought it here; for those who prepared it;
for those who cooked it; and for those who serve it.
Now we ask for your blessing on those who eat it.
Amen

973 Almighty God,
as we sit down to eat our lunch, let us remember all that
has gone into the preparation of this meal.
Help us to be aware also, Lord, of those in the world
who are short of food and water, for whom our meal
would be a feast.
Amen

974 Almighty God,
you provide for our every need.
Help us to appreciate what is now before us.
Bless this food to our use and strengthen us in your service.
Amen

975 Heavenly Father,
we are looking forward to our meal.
Let us do justice to this food, remembering that we cannot take it for granted.
Thank you for the skills of all those involved in providing our lunch today.
Amen

VESTRY PRAYERS

Before worship

976 Lord,
bless us as we go in to sing your praise;
bless us as we lead your people in worship;
and bless us as we give your Word, we pray.
Amen

977 Lord,
we pray for your presence in our worship.
Inspire our prayers and our singing,
our words and our listening.
Amen

978 Lord,
may we hear your voice
and listen to your Word
in our worship today.
Lead us, heavenly Father, lead us.
Amen

979 Bless us as we have the privilege
of leading your people in worship.
Give us good voices and cheerful hearts
as we share your Word
and sing your praise.
Amen

980 As we prepare to lead your people in worship,
help us to sing, pray and listen:
in the way you would wish,
to the standard you would expect,
and to the glory of God.
Amen

981 Thank you, Lord, for this service.
May the words and notes we sing
and the prayers we say,
enhance our worship
and reflect your word.
Amen

After worship

982 Send us out with your Holy Spirit in our hearts,
your Son's words ringing in our ears
and your will for us clear in our minds,
we pray, Lord.
Amen

983 Give us grateful hearts
as we seek to live out
what we have heard and sung today.
Amen

984 Thank you, Lord,
for all that we have sung and said.
May our worship inspire us
as we go out to do your work.
Amen

985 Thank you, Lord, for the worship
we have led in your name.
Continue to inspire us
as we go out from here
to do your will and follow your way.
Amen

986 Thank you for enabling us to lead your people in worship.
Give us grateful hearts and common purpose
to do your will and follow your word.
Amen

987 Lord, may this service inspire us
to follow your Way, your Truth, your Life,
not just today, but every day.
Amen

PRAYERS OF THANKSGIVING

988 God of great gifts,
thank you for sharing all you have
so that we may see your great works
and enjoy the fruits of your creation.
As we immerse ourselves in the busyness of the world,
help us to look up and be grateful.
Help us to slow down and be glad.
Let us rejoice at what you have done
and give thanks where thanks are due,
remembering the gift of your Son, Jesus Christ.
Amen

989 Heavenly Father,
I always come to you when I am in need,
but never when I should really thank you.
So let me mend my ways and honour your way
by giving grateful thanks for your loving kindness:
for all that makes up life in all its abundance;
for loved ones and fond memories;
for celebrations and future events;
for family and friends;
for favourite music and the arts of all kinds;
and for pets past and present.
Thank you, whose Son taught us to be grateful.
Amen

990 God of grace,
we know that your gifts are made without condition;
so the freedom we have to choose
is a gift beyond measure,
just as your creation gives infinite benefits.
However much we explore and however much
we complain,
let us be both content and searching in the way we treat
your world,
holding back where necessary and enjoying
the abundance where appropriate.
Create in us a care for the environment
as if it were your home,

because we would be honoured
if you would treat our home as always open to you too.
As Lord of the land and constant guest,
we wish to return your hospitality,
now and for ever.
Amen

991 Wonderful God,
thank you for all the friends we have,
for the fellowship and partnership they provide,
and for the sharing of joys and sorrows
that can bring both happiness and comfort.
We pray also for the friendless and rejected
in this country and many lands,
and ask that, through the love of your Son,
they may once again feel the warmth of friendship.
Help the agencies at work to restore
the spirit of community,
to be strengthened and inspired to reconnect
relationships and mend broken hearts.
We ask this in Jesus' name.
Amen

992 Lord of our joys and fears,
let me reflect, as I give thanks . . .
for what I have learned . . .
for those who have taught me . . .
for those who have listened to me . . .
for how you have loved me . . .
for where I have visited . . .
for what I have achieved . . .
for future challenges . . .
for life itself . . .
Let me grow in faith and fortitude
as I grow older.
Let me be patient and kind
as I come closer to you,
long-suffering Lord.
Amen

993 Father of all,
may we always give our thanks and praise
at the start and end of every day:
to you for watching over us;
and to your Son for dying for us.
Amen

994 Lord of great works,
as you survey your universe
we wonder at your creative love;
we are dazzled by your extravagant adventure
in sending your Son to bring us home.
Thank you, merciful Father.
Amen

995 When all seems to be against us,
you somehow turn things around.
We give you our heartfelt thanks
that you put things right in your time,
not according to our own short-sighted schedule.
May we have more faith in your plan for us.
Amen

996 For all that is, we give you thanks.
For all that might be, we hope.
For all that could have been, we have been spared.
For all that is to come, we pray.
Amen

997 Help us, Lord, to give due thanks
to those who support us daily:
through visits;
through prayer;
through deliveries;
though care;
through texting and telephoning;
through cards and letters;
through love.

Give us the strength to carry on through trial and tribulation,
knowing you are always there to guide and support us.
Amen

998 Almighty and everlasting God,
you have safely brought us to the beginning of this day.
At every rising of the sun, let us bless the Lord;
at every setting of the sun, let us thank the Lord.
With such grace abounding,
what can divide us from your love?
Amen

999 May our end of days be our hope for a bright future.
Later in life we are still children of God.
Later in life we are still in the present.
Later in life we are closer to you.
Let us rejoice and be glad.
Amen

Bibliography

Previous books by Rupert Bristow, published by Kevin Mayhew, from which many of the prayers in this collection are drawn.

Prayers for Education – a rich resource for teachers, educationalists and clergy (2005) – 1500882

Prayers for Education (2nd edition, enlarged) (2008) – 1501072

Only Connect – 150 prayers to aid reflection (2009) – 1501167

Sunday Intercessions – following the Lectionary (2010, hardback edition 2012): includes CD-Rom – 1501222

Prayers for Parishes (2011) – 1501256

Prayers for Inclusion and Diversity (2012) – 1501333

Themed Sunday Intercessions (2012): includes CD-Rom – 1501377

Services for Special Occasions (with others) (2012) – 1501340

Prayers for Saints – a biography and prayer for over 670 saints in the Anglican, Catholic and Celtic traditions (2014): includes CD-Rom – 1501445

For further details, please see our website www.kevinmayhew.com